TREATISE ON VALUES

TREATISE
ON VALUES

SAMUEL L. HART

PHILOSOPHICAL LIBRARY
New York

Printed in the United States of America

To my Wife

CONTENTS

INTRODUCTION

Almost every great thinker has been occupied with aesthetic, moral and religious values. The history of value-theories must, of necessity, become the history of philosophy.[1] Since we are less concerned with value-theories than with the value problem, as such, we will focus our attention only on those thinkers who contributed most to the solution of the following questions: Are value-notions arbitrary and adventitious interpretations of value-irrelevant facts? Are values names for simple, immediately given qualities, like color, sound, or are they generic concepts of fundamental significance? Does the undeniable fact of valuing refer to values as verifiable events? If so, what kind of subjective and objective constituents of value are there? What motives are to be found behind the artificial disjunction between values and facts? Is science value-free? Are our desires and emotions exclusive sources of values? What part does our reason play in experiencing of values? Are true value-propositions possible? Can they be experimentally tested and do they have inferential meaning? Does the shift, the evolution of values, speak for a subjectivism of values?

There is no better proof against nominalism than the functional significance of values, their role in actions and interactions, for which they stand. Were values meaningless words, we could not act upon them, our value-judgments could neither be communicable nor shareable. In spite of the "chaos of valuation" there is a great deal of agreement in all statements concerning fundamental actions and reactions. Such judgments stand for facts, affairs which can be verified. If value-notions have factual reference, why so much ado about values as entities, essences, emotional ejaculations, undefinable words? Why so many value-theories?

The same facts call for the same interpretations. But if one approaches facts with prejudices, bias, wishful thinking, no wonder that his interpretation will be different. Plato views facts with such a bias. He sees in them nothing but fleeting sense data, imperfect images of eternal paragons, ideas. Kant makes the artificial distinction between theoretical and practical reason; he speaks of two realms, the world of phenomena and the world of noumena, and entangles himself in fallacies like that of the domain of causal determination and intelligible freedom. How should a mere postulate of practical reason become a principle of our moral conduct? To ponder upon such difficulties is left to the reader's patience.

If we realize that values are not phenomena, given to our senses, but rather generic concepts which we arrive at by experiencing and comparing events, the value-problem loses all of its ominous, unsolvable character. We need only inquire whether these notions are verifiable or not, that is, examine their experimental and inferential meanings. No universal is undefinable. Undefinable are only words which stand for immediately given qualities. Values do not refer to such properties, but rather to similarities and regularities of our experiences. As universals they are neither initial as Plato would have us believe, nor final, as value-absolutists assume them to be. Finality of universals would imply knowledge of all events, actual as well as potential ones. To believe in the possibility or possession of such knowledge is absurd, to say the least. If we take value-terms, whether good, bad, beautiful, ugly or wicked, as ready-made, and as such, revealed to us by some mystical power or intuition, then we are unable to cope with the value problem. We struggle in vain to overcome artificially created difficulties. We isolate values from the context of events in which they function, we ascribe to them some intelligible existence and, later on, we try in vain to find a conjunction between values and facts. By scparating that which is not scparable we embark upon the solution of questions that cannot be solved because they are pseudo-questions. Such pseudo-questions are: the disjunction between reality and value; the division of value-free sciences and value-sciences; cosmic significance of values, etc.. No valid notions are ready-made, waiting to be grasped, and no universals are timeless, valid under all conditions. Skeptics in ethics, aesthetics, sociology, are skeptics because they once believed in phantoms and one day discovered that their phantoms were lifeless shadows. The cry for transvaluation and devaluation comes from thinkers who looked for values as eternal patterns of an absolute character. No wonder that anyone who approaches the value problem critically must first clean up the accumulated rubbish. He sees himself forced to discuss questions which are not worth arguing about. One of these is the antithesis of values and facts. Do we have such separate domains? Are facts, events, sensed and reflected upon by us as they are in "themselves"? Is not reality itself a valuative product? We no longer speak of the receptivity of the senses and the spontaneity of the intellect. We know that selectivity and spontaneity are indicative of the senses as well as of the cognitive faculties.

Another example of a pseudo-question is the cosmic significance of values. What do we mean by that? Do we ask whether forms of our life are valid for the whole universe? Such a question is naive, and, in addition, very pretentious. It reminds us of the anthropomorphic view of our remote ancestors who considered themselves centers around which all events revolved. In their endeavor to explain everything from the human standpoint they found justification for the existence of tigers and other beasts as necessary creatures for strengthening our power. Behind the "cosmic significance" of values lies our hidden inertia which clings to "eternal" values in order to throw away all responsibility in shaping our life.

The value problem becomes intangible if we erroneously aver that man, out of the blue, invented beauty, goodness and holiness, or that some divine inspiration instilled these "timeless entities" in us. An exclusively chaotic life could never inspire us to the order that is characteristic of values. Because things and events themselves have different degrees of importance, we learn to treasure them accordingly. From immediate preferences we come to deliberate, reasonable choices. By virtue of our intelligence we focus attention on objects of enduring gratification and establish a scale of values without which life could neither be sustained nor expanded. A thorough study of the facts reveals similar responses to, and uniform valuations, of fundamental issues. Primitive as well as more civilized groups show recurrent patterns of preference. Murder is always disapproved, and whenever killing is sanctioned, the victim is considered as inferior, as obsessed by a devil. A procedure not uncommon among civilized people caught in the grip of impostors and insane tyrants.

If we take sense data as valid starting points for the natural sciences, we cannot deny such a role to emotions which frame our social world. Pleasantness and unpleasantness, love and hate, attraction and repulsion, are not less indicative of objective events than sensations. Only if we take emotions as isolated occurrences, as exclusive psychic phenomena, coming and going independently of external circumstances, do we subscribe to the wrong belief that our valuative responses are mere ejaculations with no factual reference at all. Neither desires nor emotions are such isolated functions. Emotional data may deceive us, as sense data sometimes do. Whether they do so or not is a matter of verification. To verify them means to find their referential meaning. Value-notions, like all other valid universals, are social, communicable patterns. Their meaning cannot be established a priori, or decreed. Experience is the only road to valid concept; experience not limited to immediately given data. Previous experiences as well as constant inquiries into causes and effects of events, into their antecedents and consequences, must be added to find valid notions.

We have a very modest aim in this study: to clarify value-concepts, to understand their objectivity, relativity, as conditioned by shifting physical and social factors, and to comprehend that there cannot be any other court of appeal than experience adjudicated by reason. We shall expose metaphysical indulgings as plays on words, and shall point to the harm thinkers may cause by talking about absolute values as immutable essences. Such speculations are of dubious worth and usually lead to retrogression. That philosophers may become exponents of their time with all its insufficiences and disguised evils, is a well-known fact. Plato, notwithstanding his greatness, espouses the caste-system of his time. Kant, by lecturing about an ominous, "intelligible" freedom, neglected the real freedom which alone counts, freedom from fetters, freedom to grow and to expand. Man does not act morally because of some mysterious "ought of an autonomous reason." Ought judgments concern an end to be adopted in the course of action. Whenever we face difficult situattions and a choice becomes imperative, we do not ponder upon an "ought" isolated from facts, but rather reason about the course to be taken, about antecedents and consequences of an action. The ought consciousness is the "consciousness of something to be done,"[2] the ought is in the action and never has its "own justification."[3]

Kant was not satisfied with moral values, valid under certain conditions. He aspired to an absolute norm, imperative, valid under all conditions. In order to find it, he had to disregard moral conduct as fact, our emotions, desires, purposes, claims, demands, expectations, our genuine and acquired social impulses, and had to invent some fictitious realm where a pure will is supposed to reign. A pure will working against desires, emotions! What a lifeless phantom! Having once invented such an entity, Kant tries to solve moral problems, independently of experience, by making deduction after deduction from his fundamental proposition which is nothing but a petitio principii. There is, indeed, nothing good but a good will. But if this will is not to be found in our desires and the ways of their gratification, in our elated emotions, in our sympathetic responses to human misery and suffering, what is good about such a will? To remain indifferent to pain, torture, and distress of others, not to react to injustice with all emotional vigor, is callousness.

The great interest in our day for the value problem was called into life by Nietzsche's "Genealogy of Morals" (1887). Nietzsche deserves credit for bringing to the fore a problem that has been neglected, — the evaluation of values. Such evalutaion is imperative, and, if properly conducted may help to ward off social disorders. Not to take things for granted is always a sound principle. Nietzsche, by putting emphasis on the comparative and genetic approach to values, accentuates the history of values, their evolution in the course of years. If we learn to see in values historical products, we realize their conjunction with facts, events. Notions that change stand for realities. In short, a genetic approach dismisses all metaphysics of values, assumptions about values as timeless, immutable entities, divine revelations and the like. Nietzsche deserves credit for asking the right questions. He does not deserve it for the answers he gave because they are unscientific, oracular, speculative and very harmful.

Nietzsche does not start from family and kinship groups when he elucidates moral concepts, but from more complex societies where we encounter castes, classes, masters and slaves. Had he started from primitive groups, he could easily have found in them rudiments of social life— firmness, consideration, interdependence, response to pain and suffering. If we focus our attention on those fundamental facts, we find more similarities than diversities among people. The difference rests more with secondary, unimportant modes of behavior, such as manner of eating and dressing, form of companionship, custom of wooing and many other conventional habits. Once we realize that values have factual reference, that they stand for our dispositions, modes of behavior, for the ongoing interaction of environment and our own organization, then we must reject Nietzsche's division of master-and-slave morality. If the mere fact of conquest effects a transition of values, makes of a master a bearer of values and bearer of disvalues of a slave, then the value-notions must be arbitrary and adventitious. Such a conclusion is untenable, it cannot be verified. It is not true that masters consider good whatever slaves regard as bad. Both have the same fundamental moral concepts, the only difference being that the masters do not apply them to slaves.

Nietzsche contradicts himself on many points. He knows that political superiority leads to a wrong belief in mental superiority, but he nevertheless treats masters as if their mental superiority were a fact and not a deception. If masters confer higher values upon themselves, this does not mean that they possess them. Nietzsche probably believed that they did possess them, otherwise he could hardly have sided with masters against slaves. By doing so he reveals his inconsistency in thinking. If subjugation proves superiority, then why not apply it to slaves who stood up victoriously against their ruthless oppressors? Nietzsche had a very poor knowledge of heredity. Had he been better acquainted with such matters, he could hardly have spoken of a master or slave soul. Our character is not fixed from birth, but is rather the result of environmental influences, of economic, social and educational factors. Hereditary limitations are insignificant when compared with the possibilities of a favorable environment.

The etymological investigations which Nietzsche took so much pride in, reveal what people at certain times cherished and thought of as values. To infer valid meanings for our times from their value-concepts is preposterous. What would we think of a scientist who tries to explain space and time by relying exclusively on etymological research? Universals change their meaning with new discoveries, with deeper penetration into facts. To accept the values of our ancestors is to gloss over the evolution of those values in the course of years.

It is beyond the scope of this study to analyze Nietzsche's mistakes step by step. We should merely like to point out his confusion of the genetic method as a means with an end. We apply this method solely for a better foundation of present problems. The continuity of culture reveals survivals and rudiments of the past. But to believe that a knowledge of the past can provide us with solutions for our own problems is to subscribe to the wrong proposition "that the less known, or not so well known, the distant past, can serve as an explanation of the better known, the present. Psychologically, just the opposite is true."[4] The

extremely complex character of our life cannot be eluci-
dated with concepts derived from simpler forms of life.
Our necessities, aims and interests are different from those
of our ancestors. Recourse to the past has but heuristic
importance, it accentuates spiritual continuity in the historical process of the transformation of values. Because
our experiences are "intellectually cumulative" (Dewey)
we advance.

Whoever expects to find in this treatise norms of
behavior valid under all circumstances will be disap-
pointed. Just as natural science cannot guarantee harmonious, enduring happiness, no more can ethics, which
deals with human behavior, man's frailty and strength.
We experience natural cataclysms that defy our knowledge, and we face social catastrophies that make for
pessimism and despair. In such a mental state we are
all too easily inclined to discredit psychological and ethical
findings. Such an attitude is no more justified than is
the discrediting of physics because of natural calamities.
To berate knowledge means to open the door for superstition, magic, ignorance—forces which breed and perpetuate evil. Scientific findings are great assets if we learn
to avail ourselves of them. We must propagate them with
the same vigor and persistency as charlatans disseminate
errors, prejudices. If science keeps itself aloof from political chaos, from all artificially created divisions, it may,
some day, have to fight for its own existence. To disparage
its achievements because of parasites or beasts imbued
with lust for power and destruction, is to blame science for
our own lack of courage and impotence in realizing its
findings.

INTRODUCTION

The old refrain we hear so often about the unscientific character of value-judgments is the biggest fallacy of our time. If we focus our attention on fundamental forms of life, differences are rather the exception than the rule. This, we hope, our book will make apparent. It will disclose the possibilities of verifying value statements. Valuative judgments are not artefacts that we can dispense with. Inquiry into their validity is a necessity of life itself. If we go after things that turn out to be unimportant, if we trust blindly where circumspection is imperative, if we take prejudices and superstitions for truth, and bias for evidence, we may have to pay for it very dearly.

The more we know, and the better we employ reason in our passions and emotions, the better our chances for a well integrated life. If we learn to evaluate the objects of our likes and dislikes, we may cultivate friends where potentialities for friendships exist and avoid squandering our energies on a beast. No critical, experimental value approach leads to nihilism or solipsism. It shows, on the contrary, the objectivity of values in their being conditioned by many observable events. Our physical as well as our social world determine our value-judgments which, in turn, influence the former. The relativism of values accentuates their genesis and by doing so dismisses their absoluteness and, at the same time, points to their growth. A thorough study of facts directs to anticipation of new facts. Life is, to a certain degree, what we make of it. True, it imposes limitations on our aspirations, but at the same time it offers many opportunities. The relativism of values means an interrelation and interdependence of

values. With the steady increase of our knowledge, valuative judgments become better founded. So long as we
knew very little about human character we used to consider good and bad the results which an action brought
forth. With insight into character traits and their integration we draw conduct and character close together. So
long as we believed in creation as a divine inspiration we
used to talk about beauty as trance, as ineffable, ominous
quale. But if we learn to look at creation as a natural
process in which our psychic life grows through objectified expressions, we gain new means of evaluating aesthetic objects. The relativism of values makes us less pretentious. We no longer seek a perennial truth. We do not
aspire to build forever, knowing that we cannot assume
ultimacy for our findings. Relativism frees us from ortho-
doxy.

PART I

THE CONCEPT OF VALUE

CHAPTER I.

What Values Are

The problem of value is baffling if we try to solve that which we do not understand. If we look for values as phenomena, as mutable or immutable entities, we are groping in darkness. We do not know what we are asking, and not knowing our question we can never find an answer. There was a time when man indulged in similar speculations about nature. He searched for the essence of all events, for the everlasting in the flux of things, and as long as he wasted his energies on grasping some "eternal truth," his results were very poor. It was Pythagoras, one of the greatest thinkers before Plato, who realized the importance of numbers as expressive means for the relations of events. Well, we today do not ponder any more upon his speculations on numbers. We rather dismiss them as such. But about the eminence of Pythagoras' discovery that to know things means to comprehend their standing in relation to other things, to follow up their transitions,

19

there cannot be disagreement. Science began to develop with this discovery.

Whatever we know of an event is due to its interconnection with other events. To study events means to examine their transformations. If water did not freeze, nor evaporate, would not change its specific gravity, we could not have knowledge about water. What do we know about hydrogen? Well, it combines with oxygen, chlorine, fluorine; at a certain temperature it becomes a gas, at another a fluid, etc.. What do we know about mind, about reason, character, desires, emotions? We do not know them as entities, substances. We know them as events calling into being other events. We lay hold of them as causes and effects, antecedents and consequences. Because these events show regularities, because in all flux there are relatively stable elements, in all diversities similarities, we arrive at perceptions and conceptions, at meanings of events. What we conceive are not the events themselves but their meanings. "Events are present and operative anyway; what concerns us is their meaning expressed in expectations, beliefs, inferences, regarding their potentialities."[5] Meanings do not disclose the "essences" of events but rather their standing in relation to other events, their contexts. They "indicate possible interaction, not a thing in separate singleness."[6] One and the same event can partake of many meanings according to its relations. Meanings can be true or false and there is no other way of verification than by acting upon them. Dewey's "Instrumentalism" emphasises the functional role of our concepts, their importance in facilitating and directing our experiences. By accentuating the verifiability of true concepts and true propositions, Dewey widens the narrow, pragmatic definition of truth as that which is useful. Our concepts are neither "adventitious" nor "arbitrary". Whenever they stand for action and interaction, they are "results of elaborate experimental inquiry in tracing out causal dependencies and relationships." [7]

We are engaged in the process of knowledge, in perceptions, conceptions, induction and deduction for the sake of better adaptation to our physical and social environment. Behind the urge for truth is the comprehension of its value. By emphasizing the value-character of truth we are cognizant of the fact that, primarily, our concern is with efficacies and advantages of events, with occurrences in their relation to us. The study of their interconnections is intrinsically bound up with this practical interest. In order to know efficacies of events we must penetrate into the mode of their happening, into their causes and effects. The division between value-free sciences (natural sciences) and value-sciences (history, sociology, ethics) is artificial. Both deal with facts, and the only difference between them lies in the various events and their contexts they inquire into. The degree of verifiability of all judgments, factual as well as valuative ones, "is determined by the character of events of interaction."[8]

There are no purely theoretical problems. Behind each problem there is some want, interest. The prerequisite for every efficient inquiry is passion for the subject-matter we embark upon. Impartiality of scientific quests does not mean "practical disinterestedness", but rather an approach without personal prejudice, keeping aloof from wishful thinking and statements which cannot be verified. It is the depth and the breadth of the interest which count, the passion for a better humanity. The natural sciences grew out of such an interest. Psychology, sociology, ethics have their source in the same passion. If the interest for "pure truth" has any meaning at all, it denotes the will to judge critically, to avoid all generalizations that cannot be verified, not to flatter any particular social group, not to take bias for evidence. Such a scientific approach rests with our moral attitude. "The system of science (employing the term science to mean an organized intellectual content) is absolutely dependent for logical worth upon a moral interest, the sincere aim to judge truly."[9]

The comprehension of truth as value is the consequence of Kant's Transcendental Philosophy. Kant realized that our physical world as seen by the senses and apprehended by reason is a product of the continuous interaction of environment and our own organization. The underlying principles of this interaction are life-sustaining and life-furthering. Truth itself becomes in this way a value, that is, the most propitious expression of our ongoing adaptation to nature. Unfortunately, Kant himself did not follow up consistently his discoveries. Through his predilection for divisions his philosophy "abounds" in artificial disjunctions, such as "receptivity" of the senses and "spontaneity" of the intellect, "empirical" and "pure" will, "theoretical" and "practical" reason. Kant overlooks that discernment, comparison, organization, selectivity appertain to our intellect as well as to our senses; that

22

our psychic life does not contain discrete elements, like sensations, perceptions, conations and cognitions. Man acts as a unit. For methodological reasons we speak of distinct faculties, but we must not forget that they are not real divisions, that they stand for interdependent, continuous functions. If we keep this in mind, the primacy of will or intellect turns out to be a pseudo-question. The urge for unification of artificially established disjunctions is common to all Neo-Kantians. Cohen assumes a "cultural consciousness" that should guarantee the concatenation of natural and ethical sciences. Natorp speaks of the value-significance of truth. For Windelband and Rickert the value character of truth is beyond any doubt.

Windelband makes a distinction between the content of judgment and the act of judgment (Urteil and Beurteilung).[10] Whenever we judge, we bring elements together, we state their connections. The act of judging is our attitude, or assent and dissent, which express the conformity between the content judged as true and our own organization. Windelband defines truth as satisfaction of the demands of our "logical consciousness in general" (logisches Bewusstsein ueberhaupt) that has ideal validity of which ought (sollen) is the main constituent.[11] Much as Windelband tried to overcome the artificial division of theoretical and practical reason, he accomplished very little in this direction through the distinction he made between natural and historical sciences (Natur- und-Geisteswissenschaften). The former are supposed to be nomothetic, the latter idiographic. But whatsoever facts we inquire into, we do so scientifically, if we look for regularities and similarities, and explain a particular event in its whole context with other facts. Generic propositions that can be verified are the goal of all sciences, be they natural or historical sciences.[12]

Rickert brings factual and valuative judgments in close connection by putting emphasis on our active attitude of assent and consent, approval and disapproval.[13] Truth itself cannot be comprehended except under the perspective of value.[14] In describing, ordering, inquiring into causes and effects, we are not guided by some interest in "pure" truth, rather by the practical need to grasp the meaning of events in order to act upon them. Selectivity is a prerequisite of all knowledge of physical as well as of social events.[15]

Rickert regards value as the pivotal concept of our world-outlook (Weltanschauung).[16] But he does not give us a sound and verifiable analysis of the concept of value. Values, he says, do not exist, they are valid (sie gelten). We could agree with this statement if Rickert applied "valid" to generic value-notions. Concepts of value are valid or invalid; they are not immutable essences. But Rickert probably thought of values as phenomena because he ascribes to them an independent realm. He speaks of an ideal "ought" as their essential feature.[17] Once he separated values from facts he had to look for some third domain where the two could meet. This he claimed to find in our acts of judgment the objects of which are meanings (Sinnbedeutungen).[18]

If we disregard all the metaphysical speculations in which Windelband and Rickert indulged, and concentrate our attention on the comprehension of truth as value, we find that our organization plays an important part in all acts of knowledge. In the process of sensations, perceptions and apperceptions we do not go out to the things in themselves, we do not grasp essences of events, but register their regularities and connections. Valid propositions can be tested only by acting upon them; our theoretical interest is bound up with our practical interest to act in the most propitious way. In Dewey's Instrumentalism we find valid consequences of the comprehension of truth as value, free of the metaphysical implications Neokantianism was responsible for. Dewey dismisses speculations about "entities," "eternal essences" and directs us to experiences from which we arrive at generic notions. The main reason why sciences which deal with human behavior trail far behind the natural sciences lies in the wrong interpretation of value-universals. They were and are considered as ready-made and fixed, as initial and final, whereas in reality they change their meaning with our expanding. Because they express our life in its interrelation with nature and man, they are real in our impulses, habits, emotions. Because they live, "they are being corrected by unforeseen consequences or by observed facts which had been disregarded."[19] Dewey puts the main emphasis on the value of consequences. "Instrumentalism is an attempt to constitute a precise logical theory of concepts, of judgments and inferences in their various forms, by considering primarily how thought functions in the experimental determination of future consequences."[20] Instrumentalism rules out the relativism of truth and error. If the meanings of concepts are verified by actions upon them, their validity is a matter of experience. We cannot make valid inferences from errors. Nietzsche, who

25

anticipated much of modern pragmatism, overlooked this fact. "The falseness of an opinion" says he, "is, for us, no objection to it; it is here, perhaps, that our new language sounds most strangely. The question is, how far an opinion is life-furthering, life-preserving, species-preserving, perhaps species-rearing; and we are fundamentally inclined to maintain that the falsest opinions (to which the synthetic judgments a priori belong) are the most indispensable to us; that without a recognition of logical fictions, without comparison of reality with the purely imagined world of the absolute and immutable, without a constant counterfeiting of the world by means of numbers, man could not live — that the renunciation of false opinions would be a renunciation of life, a negation of life. To recognize untruth as a condition of life, that is certainly to impugn the traditional ideas of value in a dangerous manner, and a philosophy which ventures to do so thereby alone places itself beyond good and evil."[21] If Nietzsche speaks of concepts as logical fictions he only proves how deeply he himself was entrenched in the belief in the ontological character of knowledge. Concepts are not reality-cuts. To call them fictions, means to expect them to be such parts. Universals are neither fictions nor existing phenomena. They are our "intellectual tools" (Dewey) and stand and fall with their "bearing upon" our conduct, our adaptation and adjustment. Concepts have this "bearing upon" if the regularities, similarities and relations which they describe are real facts. Were our experience nothing but a sum of chaotic, isolated, fragmentary elements, the consistency and coherence our true concepts imply would be fictitious. Upon wrong generic concepts, upon wrong propositions, is neither action nor interaction. They distort every event by isolating it from its multifarious contexts. Untruth has never been life-furthering, in any field. Whenever men have been engaged in slaughter, destroyed each other, they have done it because of perpetuated errors, superstitions and ignorance.

The division between value-free sciences and value-sciences is a fallacy. On whatsoever problem we embark, value is the directing thought. Knowledge has one purpose: to find, among events, those which sustain and enhance our life. If we focus our attention on the interconnections of things, if we study their relations, we do so for the purpose of effecting a better adjustment to environment, physical as well as social. The natural sciences are not less concerned with efficacies, actual and potential, than the social sciences. Scientific findings influence our behavior, change our environment. New discoveries condition our valuations and transvaluations.

Nobody approaches a situation free of any frame of reference, free of values. The free spirit of scientific inquiry does not come to life all of a sudden. Man had to become morally mature before he could explore nature scientifically. Remove from science the moral obligation to judge truly and it becomes a caterer to social misery and injustice. What a shame that modern societies do not hesitate to appropriate immense sums for deadly weapons while poverty and hunger prevail! What a disgrace to squander natural resources on extirpation and annihilation instead of controlling them for the benefit of mankind! Not only science but also art and religion are vitiated if moral values are ignored. No great work of art has ever been achieved without passion for humanity and faith in its dignity. Mere gloating over the misfortunes of others does not make for greatness in creation. Empathy, compassion for misery and suffering do. A religious creed founded on hate, persecution, intolerance, points to moral decadence. We speak of proper and improper religion, of genuine, true art and simulated, corrupt art, and the discerning point is always a value. Behind our urge for truth is its moral import, its propitiousness from biological, spiritual and social points of view.

The Functional Significance of Concepts

The tremendous progress of the natural sciences began the moment man abandoned the ontological theory of concepts, inaugurated by Parmenides, Plato and Aristotle. Ideas, concepts, precepts were for them immutable essences of things and events. The world thought of was static, and since our senses conveyed fleeting data, they were discredited as deceptive organs. Our intellect was considered an exclusive source of true knowledge. Its role was that of an adequate mirror of ideas as eternal paradigms of reality. Once the belief in concepts as ontological notions was accepted, the making of definitions, axioms, inferences became the main task. A static world-outlook of necessity calls for rationalism, formalism. The study of facts was consequently neglected.

As long as we ascribed to our concepts an ontological significance, we thought of knowledge as an adequatio rei and considered it possible that some day we may discover the "truth in itself," an absolute eternal truth. Kant exposed this error once and for all. His Transcendental Philosophy recognizes a posteriori and a priori factors of knowledge and draws the correct conclusion that nature and mind are reciprocally determined. Kant may be wrong in his interpretation of a priori forms as initial and final constituents. In reality, they are probably results of our adaptation, and, as such, rather mutable than fixed schemes, categories and the like. But Kant deserves credit for liberating us from metaphysical speculations about an "absolute" truth. We have learned to be more modest and content ourselves with an evolving truth, conditioned by our means of studying events.

Unprejudiced inquiries into facts led to the dynamic world-outlook. Instead of indulging in the "essences," or "intrinsic qualities" of things, man began to focus his attention on the causes and effects of events, on their interconnections and transformations. A dynamic world calls for concepts different from those of a static one. With the shift of the question from "what is an event" to "how does it occur," from the objects in their "singleness" to their various contexts, the concept of substance had to be replaced by the concept of function.[22] Once we realized that the discharging and transition of energies are the only perceptible and apperceptible constituents of reality, physical as well as mental and social, the meanings of ideas and propositions stopped being attributes which we could add to, and subtract from the objects, arbitrarily. Experience became the sole arbitrator.

The significance of universals depends upon their role in facilitating and guiding our particular experiences.[23] In the case of value-notions it is not different. They are

29

neither "initial" nor "final." Like all other valid generic concepts, they are results of experiences and change with them. With values we describe events from certain perspectives. The fact that the same event may be expressed by a factual or valuative judgment shows how intimately connected they are.[24] The subject-object relation, which is characteristic of all our knowledge of events, becomes more apparent in value-judgments. The valued object and valuing subject are complementary units. The efficacies of objects are conditioned by our own responses. To assume that values are nothing but psychic effects is to believe in responses without external stimuli. All thinkers who deny the objective constituents of values disregard the whole context in which these occur. Our gratifications are not random experiences. They have causes and effects. They come from objects and are directed toward objects. Things and events must have certain properties, potentialities, in order to become the objects of our desires, emotions and evaluative thought. If our mind were an entity independent of other events, our likes and dislikes would have their order of coming and going and no external reference would be necessary. We no longer believe in such an entity. Our knowledge of psychic life is not information about mental substances. It is a knowledge of functions. So long as we thought of nature as a complex of static substances, we were at a loss to explain psychic occurrences with concepts applicable to things in their space and time dimensions. With the modern concept of matter—substance as an expression of regularities in the transitions of energies—

we no longer have to adhere to a dualism of mental and non-mental processes. Both are forms of energy. Behaviorism (Watson) did a great deal in liberating us from hypostatization of functions like volitions (to will as substance), thinking (to an intellect as entity), etc.. But it faces great difficulties in describing and explaining such facts as deliberation, choice, consciousness. There is reasonable and unreasonable behavior, showing differences which we cannot comprehend from the behavioristic standpoint. Reason stands not only for behavior but for effective behavior where the consequences of an action are anticipated. In such deliberations the value-concept is an indispensable weapon.

The concept of value permeates our life at every step. We prefer one thing to another, we shift attention from one event to another, praise one behavior and condemn another, we like and dislike, and whenever we do so, we value. Behind our passions, interests, willed actions is the belief that they are worth-while. We attach to them different degrees of importance or value. We speak of good and bad aims, noble and mean actions, beautiful and ugly objects, pious and impious intentions and deeds. Our whole life moves between attraction and repulsion. Events are alluring, enhancing, fascinating or repugnant, loathsome, obnoxious. In fact, we not only value, but are always conscious of a scale of values. We place spiritual values higher than mere biological ones, and the deciding factor in this preference is the enduring and harmonious integration, the former effect. Values may be high or low, wide or narrow, shallow or deep. In order to value we must comprehend this range.

The ever presence of "value" in all our doing and thinking explains its diverse meanings. No wonder some thinkers have suggested that it be discarded from our vocabulary entirely in order to avoid ambiguities from which misunderstandings and futile controversies spring. Unfortunately our language is not rich enough to provide us with words appropriate for each particular experience. Value is not the only word that implies various meanings. Object, subject, reality, substance, existence, just to mention a few, are of the same character. Poverty of expression is not the exclusive reason for using the same word for diverse meanings. Behind such words is a long history of emotions, images, associations, habits and customs, and the continuity of spiritual life calls for perpetuation of such expressions. After all, no science is free of concepts that have been undergoing changes in the course of years. Space and time as thought of by Newton, are not space and time as conceived of by Einstein. The causality that classical physics speaks of is not the causality which modern science applies. The same holds true of matter, mass, energy, etc.. As in physics, no harm results from employing old established concepts, provided the scientist knows their changed meaning, so in psychology, ethics and sociology the same fundamental universals can be successfully used in spite of their steady modifications. Each alteration is an incorporation of notions "as limiting concepts of a more general formulation. And so on, into future. What is significant now will be integrated into wider perspectives. That is the career of truth in our world."[25]

A complete discarding or substituting of words is feasible when they become meaningless, devoid of factual reference. With value this is not the case. It points to things, habits, actions. To find their common denominator is to arrive at the valid concept of value. With this problem are many others connected. Is knowledge of values possible? Do our immediate experiences of values lead to valid propositions? What is the nature of disagreements in valuative judgments? A critical approach to all these questions must have its starting point in experience of values.

Valuing and evaluations are facts, psychic functions occuring whenever an object or event invokes or redirects our activities. If our valuing, our immediate liking and disliking, approval and disapproval never led to disappointments and failures, evaluation would not spring into life. Evaluation occurs because our immediate responses turn out to be insufficient in comprehending objective constituents of value. Evaluation is founded on value universals. Like all other generic notions value-concepts are "intellectual tools" (Dewey) which guide our particular experiences. Whether they are the concepts of reality or goodness or beauty, they get their "logical force" as necessary implements in finding identifications, relations and correlations of individual cases.[26] By calling something real we isolate it from its "singleness" and assign to it a wider context. We do the same by designating something as good, bad, ugly, etc.. We indicate its place in a larger total. Whether we take an affirmative or negative attitude, whether we approve or disapprove, we do much more than express our feelings of pleasantness or unpleasantness, we subsume a particular case under a generic notion and thus grasp its meaning.

We apply the term value to: valuing, evaluation, the object of valuing and evaluation, the object of desire and satisfaction, purpose or end in view, actual advantages and ideal possibilities. Its deeper roots rest with biological and social determinants. No value theory can neglect these basic factors. Our conscious, immediate experience of value does not disclose its origin.[27] To find the latter we must look far back.

We cannot draw a sharp line between biological, psychological, economic and spiritual values. They are interlaced. It is not mere chance that we apply value to such apparently different things as objects which gratify our organic needs and ends which appeal to our refined senses and higher intellectual faculties. All values spring from some needs and satisfy those needs, all of them stir our emotions and conations and presuppose cognitive elements. We could never have arrived at higher values if not for our immediate preferences which, in turn, have developed to conscious, reflective choices.[28] The primary preference is determined by biological necessities. Things, events, must have certain properties to gratify our wants. To see mere psychic effects in values, means to confuse selection with construing.

The immediate preferences which we share with every living being are insufficient responses. Whenever we are emotionally attracted and repulsed, pleasure is the agent behind our attitudes. Thus far hedonism is right, but entirely wrong when applied to such higher functions as conations and cognitions. With blind preferences we could hardly have survived, still less expanded. Once reason intervened we learned the distinction between preference and choice or deliberation. Deliberation centers on the consequences of an action. Among conflicting motives we do not decide for the intenser pleasure but for that motive which invokes and directs our activities to a better adjustment and integration.

On the basis of our immediate preferences we may define value as something which stops being indifferent. Laird speaks of "the principle of natural selection" as the fundamental criterion of value.[29] This rule implies "that it is not nature for everything to be the same all at once" ... whatever matters to a thing it is value.[30] Hydrogen and oxygen, iron filings and a magnet, carbon and nitrogen, all matter to each other, and so they are values to each other. With such a wide definition of value we are barely at the threshold of a value theory. We say very little by stating that value is what matters. Besides by not restricting values to human beings we are bound to land in metaphysical speculation. Whoever finds values in all things and assumes them in subhuman and superhuman forms, disregards the main problem of a value theory: the possibility of valid valuative judgments and, with it, the separation of subjective and objective constituents of values.

Laird has to be given credit for pointing to the objective elements of value. The fact that we are attracted to some events and repelled by others cannot be explained by means of our own dispositions or organization. There must be some "requiredness" in the events themselves.[31] Our preferences, our likings and dislikings refer to something beyond them. The value is not called into life in the act of gratification. Were values created in our acts of assent and dissent, our preferences would be arbitrary, which they are not. The acceptance or rejection of objects is a matter of our needs, but the needs themselves are object-bound. Our satisfactions vary with our organization and the objects. None of them is immutable.

Value and Standard.

Whether we are absorbed in an aesthetic object or take an affirmative attitude toward a moral deed, or feel religiously elated, we are aware of an "increment" of our psychic life.[32] This enhanced activity stands in direct proportion to previous experiences which became intellectually "cumulative" (Dewey), that is, meaningful. In judging a picture beautiful, a behavior good, we do more than evince our feeling of pleasure; we apply to them generic value-notions by virtue of which these experiences are integrated, ordered, assimilated. Since we never approach a situation psychologically and socially in a primordial way, immediate responses (in the narrow sense of the word) are sheer abstractions. Even in the most elementary acts of perceiving we are guided by the past, which has built up "a fund of meanings, habits and expectations. . . ."[33]

A frame of reference is the prerequisite for any value experience. We must know what beauty, goodness and holiness mean in order to assign them to particular, individual cases. "It is only when the notion of value, that is, standard satisfaction is familiar, that it becomes possible for the individual to claim that his satisfactions are values for himself."[34] Social determinants are operative in our life whether we are conscious of them or not. They condition our primitive needs as well as our higher interests. They facilitate the transition from immediate preferences to deliberate choices by providing us with principles, standards, upon which our valuative attitudes rest. Assignment of praise, conferring of greatness, beauty, holiness, are bound up with our belief in certain standards. They may be accepted uncritically, in which case they figure as rigid, fixed rules, or they may become objects of reflective analysis and serve as heuristic principles, adaptable to modification in connection with the whole course of experience. All creation is determined by such critical evaluations. In an ever-changing world no standard can claim ultimacy, absoluteness. The wider and richer, the more inclusive standards are, the more general and pliant they become. Rigidity leads to conventionalism and finally to smugness, philistine contentment.

Value, Desires and Volitions.

If we keep in mind that things and events have different degrees of "requiredness, directedness,"[35] and that therefore our responses vary from acceptance to rejection, from enjoying and lingering to a state of loathing, repulsion, avoiding, the insufficiency of every extreme psychological approach to the value problem becomes apparent. Brentano, Ehrenfels and Meinong, notwithstanding their great efforts to grasp the meaning of value from the experience of values, have accomplished little in clarifying the value-concept. They overestimated the process of valuing, and underestimated or neglected the object of valuing. All of them saw in valuing a unique function, above the operation of the senses and the intellect. In spite of their diverse approaches, they are closely related through interpreting value as a strictly psychic phenomenon.

Brentano divides psychic life into ideas, judgments and the attitudes of love and hate.[36] The latter have affirmation and negation, acceptance and rejection in common with judgments. Judgments as well as love and hate express our active attitude toward objects, and, in addition, imply rightness and wrongness. According to Brentano there is an analogy between considering an object true and untrue and our acceptance and rejection. Whenever we are aware of something, we grasp its goodness with the right love. There is no other guarantee of the rightness or wrongness of our attitudes than our inner perception.

By speaking of the rightness of love, Brentano revives Pascal's belief in "logique du coeur." Shaftesbury, Hutcheson, Hume and Smith adhere to the same belief, with slight variations. Shaftesbury puts emphasis on the immediate intuition of our moral sense; Hutcheson and Hume see in our genuine sympathetic attitude the source of moral values; Smith accentuates the inner voice of our conscience (impartial spectator). As long as we do not recognize another valid court of appeals for value-judgments than intuition or inner perception, a scientific approach to the value problem is impossible. Intuition is private, beyond any public control. Brentano may be right in one respect. There is no such division as blind passions and emotions on the one side, and reason, as something opposite, on the other. Our emotions change, they pass from unreasonable reactions to reasonable responses. But whenever they imply rightness, they do so because thought has intervened and diverted them from ignoble, abject ends to noble aims. Rightness of love means worthiness of the loved object, and we cannot determine whether an end is desirable or not save by reasoning as to its causes and effects, antecedents and consequences. Unreflective, emotional attitudes have great limitations. They rarely "extend beyond those near to us";[37] they tend to become fixed, habitual, and, as such, nurtured by social prejudices and personal bias. If we realize that our so-called *logique du coeur* did not come to life suddenly, but rather has developed step by step, that behind the order of our emotions there are previous experiences, implanted ideas, beliefs and tendencies, valid under different conditions than those under which we live, we then apprehend how much harm may result from neglecting reason as the most effective agent in coping with new situations.

For Ehrenfels value is contingent upon desire. "We desire things not because we comprehend some ineffable quale "value" in them but we ascribe value to them because we desire them."[38] "Value is that relation between object and subject which reveals that the subject actually desires the object or would desire it should he not be convinced of its existence."[39] (Ehrenfels uses the term desire for appetite, impulses, conations or volitions). As we have already seen our immediate response has factual reference. Preferences, although blind, are not adventitious, arbitrary. They are conditioned by the requiredness of objects. When we reflect upon our volitions, of which choice or deliberation is characteristic, we cannot help but notice objective constituents of value. The object of conations does not acquire its quality value in the act of our craving for it; rather we strive for it because it has value. Ehrenfels overlooks the "particular contexts" in which desires arise,[40] their physical and social determinants. Whenever we evaluate an object of our desires, we do so with regard to efficacies of objects. Such an appreciation forces us to go beyond our desires. Ehrenfels himself is compelled to transgress his narrow definition of value as that which we desire, by admitting that there are desirable objects, that is, objects which, by virtue of their qualities, potentialities, are desired. If there are desirable and undesirable ends then we must look for objective constituents of value. Bread is not made a value at the moment of our desiring or gratification. We desire it and are gratified by it because it has properties other objects do not have. Ehrenfels forgets that the "desirable does not descend out of the blue,"[41] that previous experiences and former evaluations condition it. We learn that some objects lead to satisfaction, others not, and this fact calls for appraising. The "desirable" is the result of such estimation. Evaluated objects are not ends "entirely independent of their context in the continuum of activities."[42]

If value is entirely contingent upon desire, then we

must assume that the object of satisfaction is not a value, since "object of gratification" and "object of desire" are different as psychic phenomena. Such a conclusion is absurd. Food does not stop being desirable the moment we still our hunger. We value it on account of its properties and potentialities. Judging from objective constituents of value the desirable and that which satisfies our desires are the same. Ehrenfels is so deeply entrenched in his belief in value as a motor-affective attitude that he even denies the reality of will obstacles. Says he, "the will-act is the more intense, the greater the hindrance it must conquer... by obstruction, impediment we mean nothing else than unpleasantness that we must take in our stride to reach our goal."[43]

Many factors are fused in our conations: organic tensions, sensations, muscular movements, aim or purpose, deliberation, previous experiences which work through our impulses and habits, social determinants, etc.. If we were psychologically pristine, free of cumulative experiences, and if the situation to which we respond were isolated from the context in which it occurs, only in such case could we define value as "anything any individual desires for any reason whatever."[44] But such an instance is fictitious.

In our volitions choice is the most important factor. Whenever we make a choice, the value character of the object is subjected to deliberation. Ends are appraised as to their efficacies, potentialities. Where desires tend to blind discharges, their objects are overestimated, value is imputed to them. Such enhanced, illusionary values bring defeat, failure, dissatisfaction. Without critical estimation our social adjustment is bound to become maladjustment. Desires are too unstable, have their own temptations and caprices. They are not the right path to values. We are helped in our conations by impulses, habits, tradition, social standards. But all these assets are insufficient. We must have recourse to reflective intelligence which examines desires as to their reasonableness, inquires into the nature of ends, their causes and effects. Desire alone calls for "immediate action without thought of its consequences;" only thought looks "toward the remote end."[45]

No better founded than the desire-theory of value is the theory that value is contingent upon interest.[46] Interest is a "dominant direction of activity"[47] and, as such, presupposes value. We take interest in something because we value it, because we select it according to its importance in our adaptation and adjustment. Interest is "regard, concern, solicitude for an object."[48] To assume that value is "any object of any interest"[49] is to identify valuing, cherishing, with value itself. By caring for something we no more create its value than does the desire itself beget the value of its objective. The absurdity of deriving value from desires or interests is proved by the fact that we apprize desires and interests. This we could not do if values were identical with the objects of desire or interest. We speak of good or bad desires, noble or ignoble interests. It is the worth-character of their ends, aims, objectives, which makes for such distinction.

Value, Feelings And Emotions.

For Meinong value is contingent upon feelings.[50] If we keep in mind that feelings have no independent existence, that "each conscious state or experience is a fused unity, of which the feeling is a pervasive and inseparable part,"[51] that activity is a necessary condition of pleasantness and unpleasantness, then every attempt to derive values from feelings is doomed to failure. Unable as we are to isolate our desires from the conditions under which they occur, we are no more able to separate feelings and emotions (which are complex and strong feelings) from their broader contexts. By putting emphasis on pleasantness, the value-object is neglected as "to its place and effects, its connection with other things."[52] Meinong is aware of the referential meaning of our emotions, and includes judgments as a necessary presupposition of every value experience. Value-feelings, says he, differ from ordinary feelings through "existential judgments." But Meinong fails to elucidate the role of thought in our value experience. Very little is gained from his distinction between object and objective. Object refers to all things, to existing as well as to "subsisting" (bestehen). Objectives are "entities" before our mind, which find an expression in statements such as "the horse is white," "the tree is green," etc.. Value-judgments are of this kind and are divided into "dignitatives" and "desideratives" according to whether they concern emotions or desires.

Emotional factors are important in our value experience, but it is ultimately our reason which makes for its adequacy. If we do not respond to cruelty with unpleasantness and to kindness with pleasantness, we will never grasp the disvalue of the former and the value of the latter. But we should not forget that we respond

43

immediately because previous experiences and prior thinking influence our direct responses by means of firm habits. Dewey is right when he considers most of our immediate appreciations as of greater psychological than moral import, "since they are indications of formed habits." They receive moral significance with intervention of reason which goes beyond our immediate responses. Our sensitiveness is enriched by all-pervading thought. The broader and more inclusive our intellectual orbit, the more elated and the more profound our emotional attitude.

The Fallacy of Hedonism.

Man is an acting being. Pleasantness and unpleasantness are epiphenomena and not motives of psychic functions. There is no other reason for acting, discharging of energies, than growth, expansion. We do not act because of pleasure. Rather, because we act, we experience pleasure or displeasure. Hedonism converts these contingent, emotional occurrences, which are results or effects, into causes. It fails entirely to describe and explain our volitions. In our willed actions anticipated objects are not feelings or emotions, but "ends in view." (Dewey). While reflecting upon conflicting motives we do not estimate future pleasures, we adjudge the outcome of actions, their moral import. In such considerations values are vital implements. They do not generate our activities, but direct and redirect them.

There is but slight disagreement about values as fulfillment of physiological necessities. Above these necessities, in all ends wherein our mind takes an interest, various attitudes are not rare. They are common because our de-sires, impulses, emotions, habits, senses and cognitive abilities must be cultivated in order to grasp higher values. If a person responds to jazz rather than to clas-sical music, if an individual hardly distinguishes between legality and morality of conduct and gets along with rigid, conventional rules, we are inclined to take this fact as proof of a subjectivism of values. We do not do so in subjects dealt with by natural sciences. No matter how insignificant the number of those who can comprehend the theory of relativity, we do not question its validity. With valuative judgments we must do the same. There are values requiring refined senses, deep sympathy and a great intellectual capacity. Where these conditions are given, disagreement in valuative judgments turns out to be exceptional.

If we reflect upon the physical embodiments of values, in art, morality, religion, we do not ponder on the pleas-ure they invoke. We focus our attention on the expressed subject-matter, on the appropriateness of the form. Man does not create pleasures. He creates works of art which differ as to the richness of life they objectify, as to their communicable meanings, as to their social functions. A painting is not beautiful because it stirs emotions, but on account of its aesthetic qualities, such as consonant color distribution, lively and sympathetic representation. A good man is not good because he offers us enjoyments. He is appreciated as good by virtue of his harmonious integration, social impulses, dispositions, fairness, sensi-tivity to misery and suffering, and his endeavor to eradi-cate them. If we look upon value as identical with pleasure, we arrive at the absurd conclusion that beauty lies in our response and not in the object; that goodness lies in the recipient of good deeds and not in the doer.

Whenever we describe and explain natural events, the underlying question is "How do they happen?" We are accustomed to making an exception in the case of man. We are not content with the discovery that the discharge of energies is as significant of human beings as it is of all other natural things. We look for some prime cause of our behavior. We ask, "Why do we act?" Out of such speculations pleasure was chosen as the exclusive motive. But desiring, striving, thinking do not stop with gratifications. We are always driven by passions, interests. Life is ceaseless activity, transformation of energies, change. From the biological as well as from the spiritual standpoint we are always in motion. Stableness is non- existing. Because imbalance is "a permanent concomitant of living,"[53] we act, we create. If pleasure were really what man is craving for, he would, of necessity, avoid any disequilibrium, which is neither possible nor desirable. Not possible, because life is action, transition and the main factor behind this continuous activity is the incessant disturbance of an effected balance; not desirable, because out of felt tensions come man's highest achievements. If we were nothing but hedonistic creatures, we would not dig out problems whose solutions require sacrifices, endurance, suffering. We would still be on the same mental level as were our remote ancestors. We have advanced because we have stopped taking things for granted and have given up smugness, indulging in transient, dubious pleasures. True happiness comes from our enhanced spiritual activities. Knowledge is a vigorous solace only for those who take in their stride the pangs and discomforts which true, unbiased thinking entails. The bliss that follows fairness and kindness toward mankind springs from our sympathy for our fellow men. How could we ever enjoy a generous deed if this deed were not the result of a struggle, of obstacles which had been overcome? No great work of art falls into the lap of its creator without the many hardships and renunciations that creation exacts. If we desire to share in his enjoyments, we must encompass all his life, which finds expression in his work. When we read about a great deed of man, we derive pleasure from it to the extent that we are able to live through all the events which brought it about. If we want to know the bliss of love we must accept its tragic vicissitudes. We do not grow and expand by pleasures, but by activities which invoke pleasures.

Value And Cognitions.

"To value means two different things: to prize and appraise; to esteem and estimate. I call them radically different because to prize names a practical, non-intellectual attitude, and to appraise names a judgment. That men love and hold things dear, that they cherish and care for some things and neglect and condemn other things, is an undoubted fact. To call these things values and then import into them traits of objects of valuation, meaning valuated objects the traits which things possess as held dear, is to confuse the theory of judgments past all remedy."[54]

Our immediate, emotional responses do not disclose the

value of the objects. We simply like or dislike, accept or reject, admire or abhor. The assertion that something is enjoyed is an exclamation of our feeling, no judgment at all. Value statements refer to something beyond our liking at the present moment; they concern the objects of our emotional attitudes. Thought goes out to relations, to meanings of inferential function. Valuative judgments do not differ in this regard from factual judgments. Through the intervention of thought our value experience becomes more adequate. If we know what art aims at, its limitations and possibilities, we are better equipped to evaluate it. We respond to certain acts with pleasure, but it is thought that teaches us to consider the single deed in its whole context, to lay hold of its agent, to understand the conditions of its occurrence and to look ahead to its consequences.

Valuing is an immediate, emotive response, evaluation is a mediate, cognitive act. As in economic goods so in all other values, appraisal is bound up with thorough knowledge. It takes long training in, and a comprehensive study of, painting, composition, writing to estimate aesthetic values. The same is true of moral and religious values. If we do not know how character works, we may like or dislike a mode of conduct, but we can never grasp its value. There is tartuffery, bluff and genuine kindness. We cannot distinguish both, unless we penetrate deep into human behavior. Our emotions are a tremendous asset in our responses to values, but devoid of reason they are dumb, inchoate, in constant danger of being attached to ignoble ends.

Valuing and evaluation complete each other. Estima-

THE CONCEPT OF VALUE

tion, when unbiased and founded on facts, rather enhances than distorts our emotive attitudes. There is no difference in this respect between a work of art, a scientific achievement and a moral or religious deed. Our sensitiveness and our erudition condition each other. Ignorance is back of all chaos in judgments of value. In matters of value there is nothing which resists impartial and scientific inquiry. Only neglect of such procedure leads us to the false belief that intuition or brute force is the final judge in values. Such belief is the greatest travesty of facts. It has its source in our inertia, which shuns all critical investigation. Inveterate prejudices, founded on hate and hostility, make us dogmatic, blind.

Value and Principles.

Our particular value experiences have common characteristics. Similar qualities, recurrent patterns, likeness of causes and effects, of antecedent and subsequent elements, call for generic concepts, universals. Such notions have no independent status. Derived from experience, they find in it their significance and sole justification. Because the conditions of our life change, physical and social environment both undergo steady transformation, our value universals are not fixed, immutable, absolute. Whoever takes them for timeless, renders "men satisfied with existing states of affairs" . . . and regards "the ideas and judgments they already possess as adequate and final."[55] Most confusion comes from ignoring the heuristic importance of value universals. If we think of them as existing general phenomena and not as instrumental, reflective tools, we are bound to indulge in useless speculations about some intelligible, perfect realm of values, or, not finding generic value phenomena, to deny all experimental and inferential meaning of our value judgments. General ideas are not valid through depicting general situations and affairs adequately, but as abstract guiding factors in comprehending individual cases. Like all other universals, value-notions are subject to further generalizations which lead to principles. Valid value principles are valid conduct principles. They help us to go beyond immediate situations and serve as directing points of view in in our estimation and deliberation.

Knowledge that keeps abreast of new findings and discoveries has valuative implications. It discloses common impulses, affections, similarities of motives and responses, genuine and acquired sociality. It reveals moral, aesthetic and religious facts which make for valid principles. Principles are not commands or rules of conduct. Ethics and aesthetics fail as normative sciences, since norms or rules applicable to all cases cannot be experimentally established. Scientific ethics and esthetics reveal valid principles as reflective methods, as intellectual implements in apprehending particular experiences. They are indispensable in our conduct, which requires steady reflection and looking ahead. Such principles in morality are fairness, justice, kindness, etc.. They guide us in adjusting our own volitions to those of others. In aesthetic evaluations "sympathetic representation," "moral and intellectual communion," "unity in variety" figure as valid principles.

Principles as intellectual instruments are flexible. There would be no creative morality, creative art or creative religion if we took principles as rigid, final rules. Whoever does it forgets that our main concern is "increase of knowledge" and not "its possession." (Dewey). Value principles are means for judging values and not values in themselves. If we disregard their instrumentality and consider them as "intrinsic values," as "ends in themselves," we are bound to land in formalism and rationalism, and to have recourse to metaphysics in answering accrued pseudo-questions referring to "reality and value," "existence and validity" (Sein und Gelten), "variable goods and invariant values" (Gueter and Werte), etc.. By declaring principles independent of, and superior to, experience, we are in danger of worshipping forms which, separated from reality, become obsolete and may turn into obstructions and unsurmountable barriers to all advance. Simmel calls this transformation of principles from means to ends the "transition to idea" (Wendung zur Idee) and sees in it a metaphysical phenomenon of our spiritual life.[56] We have a more prosaic name for it. It is human indolence coupled with ignorance, intolerance and implacability which make for rigid adherence to obsolete, meaningless forms of life.

Value And Ideals.

Man is a transcending being.[57] Never content with given states of affairs, he conceives ideas of better, more propitious forms of life. Out of such cravings culture developed. Life is activity, and activity, as Whitehead says, is emergence into future. To be concerned with the future means to dwell in possibilities and potentialities. "A particular ideal may be an illusion, but having ideals is

51

no illusion. It embodies features of existence. Although imagination is often fantastic, it is also an organ of nature; for it is the appropriate phase of indeterminate events moving toward eventualities that are now but possibilities. A purely stable world permits of no illusions, but neither is it clothed with ideals."[58] What ideals we anticipate, in what possibilities and potentialities we dwell, depends upon our mental and moral dispositions. Men of strong will who can take all hardships in their stride, crave for other things than do men of weak will. The hopes of the former are close to reality, and hence can be materialized. The hopes of the latter are more or less illusive, and doomed to failure. Like their creator, these hopes are frail and unstable. When failure follows failure, disappointment follows disappointment, we are much inclined to look for some external cause and to disclaim all responsibility. This state of mind may offer some relief for a short time, but in the long run it must have devastating effects and leads to complete defeatism. Under such conditions we are prone to heed raven black pessimists who tell us about the disjunction between value and reality, and who depict life as a brute, chaotic, senseless, hazardous affair.

There is no better evidence against any separation of values and facts than the existence of human society. Only organized life survives and expands; and organized life points to values as real, vital patterns which find expression in our impulses, habits, character or conduct and in all the arrested moments of life of the communicable and shareable work of art. Patterns of life are constantly modified. Whoever claims ultimacy for forms of life valid under certain conditions, does violence to our prospective nature, to our indomitable will to surge ahead. In the realization of ideals man restricts himself. He blames everything but himself for social evils. Instead of substantiating his aspirations step by step, in close connection with given facts and opportunities, he conceives of them as ready-made, fixed ends, waiting to fall into his lap as a gift from heaven. He shifts his responsibility to some supernatural power and deludes himself with an "eternal world order." He falls in with the wrong belief that human behavior is beyond scientific inquiry, and consequently beyond remedy.

We like to speak of social crises as irreparable and unexplainable cataclysms. Are they in reality such phenomena? Men do not engage in slaughter on impulse. Bloody battles are prepared by impostors, ruthless tyrants or demagogues who capitalize on ignorance and pseudoscientific slogans about "race superiority," "hereditary inequality," "the pugnacity of man," etc.. Not less guilty are intellectual dreamers who hypostatize their wishes and illusions into existent entities. Illusions are fancies, but ideals are objects of our planned, deliberated will-actions. Whether they are workable or not depends upon their concatenation with reality. A thorough study of facts discloses new opportunities, new possibilities. All advance, no matter in what field, is bound up with our belief in ideals.

CHAPTER II

WHAT VALUES ARE NOT

A. Values Are Not Phenomena, Essences, Entities.
(Critique Of Value-Realism).

Value and worth are often used as synonyms. In economics they denote an equivalent in money or goods. There we distinguish value in use and value in exchange. (Smith). The former describes the usefulness of things, the latter the rate of exchange. Some thinkers would like to limit "worth" to moral attributes, like excellent, outstanding, and apply "value" to economic goods. This distinction is very artificial and not feasible at all. Value is employed as noun, verb and adjective, and this characteristic makes it more suitable for moral, religious and aesthetic experiences. To value means to like, to hold dear, to cherish; in addition, value refers to those properties of things and events which invoke our valuative attitudes. Furthermore, value also stands for evaluation, appraisal, estimation, critical inquiry into the factual foundation of our likes and dislikes. These three meanings of value are often confused. If we do not keep them separate, we may be baffled by questions which we do not understand. When asking "What is beauty?" we must know whether we are concerned with our enjoyment of aesthetic objects or with properties of those objects, or whether our valuative judgment can be verified, that is, whether it has experimental and inferential meaning.

Another problem that needs clear specification is the objectivity of values. This question means: are values private experiences of single individuals, or can they be shared by many? Can we proceed from particular value experiences to generic notions, propositions applicable to future experiences? Our experience of values points to such universals. Whatsoever value we are absorbed in, we subsume a particular case under a generic concept that figures as an intellectual tool "for the express purpose of facilitating and employing our individual experiences."[59] From generic concepts we arrive at connections between them which we may bring to a common denominator. So for instance, if we ask what value in general means, we look for attributes pertaining to all values. It is not by pure chance that we apply value to such apparently different objects as economic and spiritual ends. By speaking of economic, aesthetic, moral and religious values, we stress their difference. By employing the same word "value" we accentuate their comparative properties.

To have value is not identical with being a value. We must not confuse these two meanings. If we say that a certain poem has value, we emphasize its specific properties, such as unity of form and content, melodious expressiveness, etc.. If we say that a certain poem is a value, we involuntarily look for some total "value phenomenon." A poem consists of words. Consisting of words, however, is not its value. A poem has rhymes. Rhymes alone do not constitute its value. It is written on paper; but being written on paper or printed, is not a necessary component of its worth either. No thing or event has value as a whole, with all its qualities. It has value only partially. To evaluate an object means to reflect upon its properties in terms of the sustenance and enhancement of our life. What an event does, what consequences follow from its occurrence, these comprise our knowledge of its value. Neither motives nor deeds are good or bad in isolation. Their value depends upon the whole context of events, antecedent and subsequent.

To have value is to have properties whose meanings we grasp in acting upon them. Things and events have different efficacies. They are useful or useless, furthering or retarding, fulfilling or frustrating. These functional qualities cannot be comprehended unless related to subjects. Value always implies a relation.[60] Object-subject determination or object-subject compresence (Alexander) is the main characteristic of our most generalized concept of value. Neither this universal, nor any particular value-notion has a mode of existence independent of experience. Value-realism, of which Plato is the typical representative, arrives at such an untenable conclusion. In our time Scheler and Hartmann have revived his theories. Behind Plato's value-realism stands the ontological aspect of knowledge. Its true objects are ideas, thought of or intuited as generic, existent essences. Plato not only hypostatized our concepts, but, what is more, he ascribed to them a higher reality, and regarded all things and events as mere phenomena, deceptions of the senses. The ideas are beyond all change, eternal paradigms, independent of the apperceiving subject. When one of Plato's pupils objected that we can only see particular things, e.g. a certain horse but never a generic horse, Plato retorted that he has no proper faculty for seeing ideas. This ability to him is intuition. If intuition stands for the immediate application of acquired knowledge, then it is a fact. The more we know, the easier we grasp relations, correlations, regularities, familiar patterns. Our inference becomes habitual. If intuition denotes mystic revelation, emotional insight and the like, then we must dismiss it as fictitious.

Studies of facts, inquiries into their causes and effects, lead to generic concepts which do not have an existence of their own. They are "neither initial nor final. They are the bridges by which we pass from one particular experience to another; they are individual experiences, put into such shape as to be available in regulating other experiences."[61] Plato assumes that generic notions or ideas are initial and final, that they are neither derived from nor alterable by experience. Scheler and Hartmann do the same. For both, values are timeless entities, valid under all conditions. Valuational errors are due to our blindness to values. In order to overcome this blindness we must steep ourselves deeply in a "phenomenological intuition" that alone discloses all the eternal, invariant entities that good, evil, holy, wicked, beautiful, ugly depict. To intuite these ominous, indefinable, felt "quales," we must abstract them from facts, from all events to which they refer. It remains a puzzle how we can ever have an experience of "good" that is not a particular action in which certain character traits are manifested, and unique results effected. Whenever we experience

57

values, physical embodiments or expressive forms are pre-conditions.[62] From individual cases we arrive at universals which evolve in connection with experience. To assume them as final comes close to a denial of all creativeness in art, morality and religion. Creation is not the revelation of everlasting, mystical entities, intrinsic ends of a transcendent, intelligible realm. Rather is it a discovery of forms of life, a selection by virtue of their propitiousness. Ever-changing conditions call for the transformation of ideas, principles, universals. No genuine reflection upon value-notions is of any use, unless we examine them as to their experimental and inferential significance. We cannot decide a priori, once and for all, upon values. The validity of values as well as of all other universals is a matter of experience. Einstein did not discover the new concepts of space and time by mere reflection or intuition, but only because he was unable to describe and to explain new scientific findings through Newtonian principles. The latter turned out to be inconsistent with other valid propositions.

To appeal to emotional intuition in matters of value is to perpetuate chaos of valuations. Emotional intuition is private, dogmatic, beyond critical examination. Every charlatan could take recourse to intuition if the latter were the final court of appeal. How should we ever test different intuitive results? By means of our own intuition? If concepts, judgments have any meaning at all, then they must be brought down to perceptive data. There is no distinction in this respect between value-judgments and factual judgments. Judgments without referential meaning are senseless or mere emotional expressions. Be-

fore we embark upon the second extreme, value-nominalism, let us permit Scheler and Hartmann to speak for
themselves: "There are genuine and true value qualities
which constitute an independent realm of objects . . . they
are distinctly felt objective values. We cannot define
them, we can only point to proper examination of our immediate emotional experience of good and evil."[63]

"Values can neither be created nor destroyed . . ."[64]

Scheler does not recognize a change of values but only
a shift of "goods." After having made this artificial and
untenable division of "goods" and "values" (Gueter und
Werte) he embarks upon a metaphysical exposition of the
value notions. (Imitating Kant's metaphysical exposition of space and time.) Says he, "goods presuppose the
value concepts, therefore, the latter must precede the
former."[65]

"In their mode of existence values are Platonic ideas."[66]

"There is continuous unfolding of new ethical value-
concepts. No transvaluation of values, but a revaluation
of life. In the revolution of the ethos, the values themselves do not change. Their nature is timeless, super-
historical. But the consciousness of them evolves."[67]

Behind the revival of Platonism by Scheler and Hartmann there are two motives: the urge to escape the sub-
jectivistic and solipsistic predicament of an exclusively
psychological approach to the value problem (Brentano,
Ehrenfelds and Meinong)[68] and the desire to overcome
the insufficiencies of Kant's formalism in ethics. Unfortunately the result has turned out to be of very dubious
worth. With values as felt "quales," timeless essences,
entities, we are as far away from valid judgments as we
were with values as expressions of desires or emotions.

Instead of Kant's formal definition of good (as that which ought to be) we are provided with a similar one. Good is what we intuitively grasp or feel. In order to make valid propositions we are directed to "right intuition." Such an insight is expected to lead us to the eternal values, and once we grasp them we cannot help but act in their spirit. If values are supposed to be transcendent entities of an ideal existence, why designate emotional intuition as the only competent method for their discovery? Intuition, it seems, is a very convenient escape from disturbing problems. By appealing to it we need not concentrate our efforts on experimental testing, logical inferences. We are free to indulge in all kinds of speculation. Intuitionists forget that behind their "intuitions" there may lurk bias, superstition, social prejudice, as the case of Plato shows. He acquiesces in the social divisions of his time, and adheres to castes in his "ideal state." Here we find philosophers, warriors and laborers. Only philosophers are supposed to possess the divine gift of intuiting supertemporal, perfect ideas.

B. *Values are not mere ejaculations of feelings or "commands in a misleading grammatical form."*[69]

Value-realism is untenable. Values are not objective "quales," Platonic ideas, perfect, absolute entities. No less untenable is value-nominalism that degrades values to meaningless words or subjective, emotional exclamations. Both extremes exhibit the same mistake. They consider values isolated from facts, from the whole context of the events in which they are valid. For value-realists our experiences are too precarious for absolute values. For value-nominalists only sense perceptions and memory data from previous sensations are the main source of knowledge; and since emotions are constituents of our immediate value experiences, value propositions are regarded as senseless, devoid of every experimental and inferential significance. Value-nominalism, like nominalism in general, overlooks the fact that words gain meaning "by virtue of their interaction and association."[70] Even an emotional expression as soon as it "establishes a genuine community of action" is meaningful and refers to facts.[71]

Logical positivists consider valuative judgments unscientific because of their belief that they cannot be verified. This belief is not based on facts. Judgments of value vary from other judgments "in the specific material they have to do with, in respect of method of inquiry, test, verification they do not differ."[72] If judgments of value are results of experimental inquiries and logical conclusions, they are valid, that is, they can be verified. The reciprocal determination "of the act of judging and the content judged"[73] is not an exclusive criterion of value-statements. It holds true of all judgments. Whether we are concerned with factual or valuative judgments, our impulses, habits and interests are ingredients we cannot dispense with. The division of value-free and value-sciences is, as could be seen in our previous chapter, artificial. "Disinterested knowledge" is non-existent. Behind our study of the interconnections and relations of things, behind our descriptions and explanations of events, is the vital urge to grasp their efficacies in sustaining and enhancing our life.

Physical findings condition our moral conduct. Our moral conscience determines the amplitude of our problems, the inclusiveness of our interests, our undaunted will to go beyond given achievements. There is a dynamic interrelation and interdependence of all values, theoretical as well as practical. Whatever science we reflect upon, this reciprocity is undeniable. Physics cannot dispense with psychological findings, neither can psychology get along without physical discoveries. Valid psychological propositions are bound up with valid physical propositions.[74]

Customs, standards, general ideas and principles evolve in connection with our whole experience. They have neither an independent mode of existence nor a mysterious order of transition. Our remote ancestors were not less "value-conscious" or more "value-blind" than we, to judge from their world-outlook. The facts they knew were simple, limited in space and time, isolated from each other, and related to elementary needs. Such a narrow and restricted mental orbit called, of necessity, for primitive conduct.

Scientific findings are useless if we do not avail ourselves of them. The value of the theoretical lies in its practical implications. Where there is a wide gap between knowing the right and doing the wrong, there too, we observe symptoms of maladjustment and disintegration. Moral and mental aberrations go hand in hand. "Value-blindness" and ignorance are closely related. Do we need a better proof of the fallacy of the disjunction between facts and values, between judgments of fact and judgments of value than their undeniable reciprocal determination? Could we, today, respond to an artistic work that espouses the beliefs and tendencies of our remote ancestors? Could we attune our impulses to patterns of thinking and acting valid under different conditions than those under which we now live?

If our values are nothing but mere emotional ejaculations or meaningless words (word-designata), as logical positivism wants us to believe, nihilism and scepticism must consequently follow.[75] Life does not permit of such an attitude. Without preference and deliberate choice we cannot exist. A consistent skeptic or nihilist must keep himself aloof from all approval or disapproval, from all judgments concerning the degree of importance and the efficacies of the objects he is absorbed in or deals with. Such indifference indicates nothing but mental derangement and moral callousness. Life is activity, and hence moves between inhibition and exhibition, between attraction and repulsion. Cognitive elements are indispensable factors in our actions. Mere ejaculations of feeling can neither direct nor redirect them, can neither engender nor justify claims, neither sustain nor expand social life. The most extreme value-nominalist cannot help but choose his friends, make a distinction between noble and mean motives, enduring and transient ends, evanescent and lasting interests. And the guiding principle in all these attitudes is value. Behind the comprehensive and arduous scrutiny of logical structure that analytical positivists set upon, is there not the moral precept to judge truly, the noble motive to liberate us from the vagueness of concepts and the accruing pseudo-questions?

What is the nature of the arguments of logical positivism against the scientific character of value-judgments?

They have their source in our emotional responses; they are bound up with an habitual frame of reference; they cannot be traced down to perceptive propositions; they are misguided commands or rules of action; they cannot be translated into what the positivists deem the only scientific, physical language. All these objections are artificially construed. Crude sense data, sensations and recollections of previous experiences frame our physical world. Science stands or falls with the possibility of arriving at valid generic concepts and connections between them drawn from sense data. The building up and selection of universals is not an arbitrary process. Similarities and regularities of experiences are preconditions of generic notions. Universals do not depict general phenomena, entities or essences. Their significance is a functional one. They are our "intellectual tools" (Dewey) for the sole purpose of facilitating particular experiences. Value concepts do not differ in this regard from other universals. Whenever we employ universals, we judge. Judgments, as acts of attention, involve a selective interest, motives in choosing the subject matter, and motives in the correct use of all available valid propositions and methods.[76]

Emotional data are the starting points for our knowledge of human behavior and human relations, furthering and retarding character traits, propitious and adverse forms of social life. They refer to external events, just as our sense data do. There is no logical ground for ascribing this relation to the latter and for denying it to the former. Valuative attitudes are not fortuitous occurences; they are determined, and show regularities and similarities and, by virtue of these properties we arrive at value-concepts which share their hypothetical character with all other universals. Finality, ultimacy of generic notions, would exclude all new experiences.

The frame of reference is not an exclusive quality of value-judgments. Our own organization plays an important part in framing our physical, scientific world. There is no such thing as a disinterested approach to nature. Our impulses, habits, interests, needs are lively ingredients in our cognitive functions. The value object is still less indifferent, since it is more intimately allied with our character dispositions. The objectivity of value-judgments stands or falls with our ability to get rid of personal bias, prejudices, implanted and blindly accepted beliefs. Like our aesthetic faculty, our moral and religious sense can be cultivated. The study of the objectified forms of value, inquiries into the causes and effects of value objects, penetration into character traits, looking beyond immediate enjoyments, — these are the most effective means of raising our values from "ejaculations of feelings" to valid propositions of inferential significance.

So long as we mistake value-notions for phenomena, we hunt in vain for such perceptive data. Value-concepts are generic ideas whose meaning we grasp by acting upon them. Their validity depends upon their fulfillment of our anticipations, beliefs, expectations. If we assume universals as independent of, and superior to, individual cases, and isolate them from the whole context of experience, they become lifeless, rigid, and finally meaningless.

Valuative judgments are neither true nor false for logical positivism. It arrives at this absurd conclusion by misinterpreting value propositions as commands in a misleading grammatical form."[77] "From the statement, 'Killing is evil', we cannot deduce any proposition about future experience."[78] Carnap does not see any difference between the expression "Do not kill" and "Killing is evil." In reality they differ immensely. "Killing is evil" is a concise expression of our knowledge about human character and social behavior; its meaning can be decided by action upon it. Behind this statement are valid psychological, ethical and social propositions. The road, as Dewey puts it, from any valid universal to particular cases leads through habits, impulses and intellectually "cumulative" experiences. To infer propositions about future experiences from a judgment of value, we cannot approach it psychologically, mentally and morally "pristine." The more general a statement is, the more knowledge it requires for its comprehension. Such a judgment cannot be considered detached from other statements, less general, which can be traced down to perceptive data. In this respect there is no difference between judgment of value and judgment of fact.

Carnap speaks of the unity of science and recognizes "physical language" as the only scientific one. True statements, says he, are those that can be translated into space and time relations. Biology, psychology, sociology and ethics are sciences only to the extent that their propositions can be translated into physical terms. But "scientific" stands for a critical method of experimental testing and inquiry and, hence, can be employed in any field. Verification concerns the validity of a judgment and not its physical nomenclature.

PART II

CHAPTER III

VALUES AND THE CREATIVE PROCESS

There is no fundamental difference between creative men and non-creative; the distinction is only one of degree. Were creativeness something metaphysical, irrational through and through, an exclusive gift of a few outstanding individuals, their creations, given in objective forms, could never become a common good. Values are shareable, communicable, because all of us are able to experience them, that is, to recreate them, to make their life a part of our own life. Our experience of values can be adequate or less adequate. The grade of adequacy depends upon our abilities, our developed perceptual, emotional and cognitive faculties, our will to transcend the narrow bodily self and to actualize the higher, richer, social self which finds in the spiritual values not only an expression but a source of new energies, new stimuli.

The experience of values involves much more than skill and technical knowledge. We must have an intimate relation to the subject matter which finds expression in a created work and grasp the ultimate goal of the creative process. Science remains a system of abstract concepts

67

and sentences if we are not driven by the passion of learning, and are not imbued with the fervor of a better social adjustment. Music will hardly appeal to us if we do not realize that our common nature, that our emotional gamut, finds an expression here. If we do not look for life revealed in a picture or sculpture, we may enjoy the shape of colors or lines, but the objectified value will remain a closed book for us. Man does not create merely to reflect actual life with its good and evil, justice and injustice, but is always inspired by a loftier aim. This aim is a richer and more dignified humanity which he hopes to actualize by pointing to better adjustments and integrations of our will with the will of others.[79]

Values do not descend upon us as a gift from heaven. They are not given in the universe as static, sublime entities, essences which we intuit. Rather, we create them; and as our own designs and discoveries, they mirror our frailty and strength, our shame and glory, our wants and satisfactions, likes and dislikes, griefs and joys. Because we are both inert and active, progress becomes an infinite task. With each value we must conquer some disvalue. The history of mankind is full of scientists, painters, sculptors, poets, but at the same time full of impostors, tyrants, criminals.

By creating values man reveals himself as a spiritual being who finds the essence of his existence in continuous activity. Where there is action, there too, is felt a disequilibrium and a tendency toward equilibrium. Pleasure, the resulting emotional tonic of each equilibrium, is not the final goal. The greatness of a work of art lies not in the invoking of pleasure, but rather in the stirring of our whole psychic life by pointing to our shortcomings and new opportunities. Smugness and complacency are incompatible with greatness. With the dawn of his mind, his spirit, man expands his horizon in many ways. He becomes self-transcending, able to grasp a wider world than the reality of his senses, make the past a part of his present and finally unite his personal life with a larger and richer life in the course of his social development.[80]

Each self-transcendence has as its epiphenomenon pleasure. But to assume that enjoyment is the ultimate objective of all creation is entirely wrong. By doing so we close our eyes to the fundamental fact that our mind is that which stirs new dissatisfactions. It is true that as spiritual beings we become aware of the many opportunities for a better life, but we cannot deny that the same mind makes our suffering more intense. Our pleasures and displeasures increase with the growth of our spirit. Sickness, death, cataclysms of nature, the steady flux of things and events, the innumerable evils nature has in store for us, and the evils caused to men by men themselves, become a source of intense suffering in the moment they enter conscious life. As psychic phenomena, as transformed by perceptions, conceptions, emotions, conations, they ingrain themselves in our memory and begin to endure. Could we live exclusively in the present, without a past and a future, reality could not become a source of suffering, and certainly not the source of intense pleasure which creative life invokes. Its bliss springs from the inclusiveness of our acting in grasping, forming and molding reality. This process is unending, since each actualization calls for new potentialities.

In a world itself pregnant with values, in a completely perfect environment, full of harmony, creation would not be necessary. As thinking is being called into life, "as response to discomfort, to pain, to uncertainty, to problems such as could not exist in a world made for us,"[81] so painting, writing, composing. Behind our will to construction there is always a felt and comprehended insufficiency. Creation would be impossible, too, in a world completely incongruent with our wants and ideals. If we could not realize values, we could not endure those "death and birth pangs" which creation entails. To a certain extent man is master of his own fate, at least in respect to environmental circumstances which are conditioned by man himself. His creative abilities here turn out to be a tremendous asset.

The creative process is a complicated action in which our whole psychic life grows. With any expression we not only give sensations, emotions and thoughts palpability, but enhance their activity to the utmost by effecting an enduring and harmonious interaction. The more perfect this inner process of integration is, the more appealing the subject matter represented. Our experience will have moments similar to the creative process itself. It will show proportion and balance, cohesion, consistency, coordination and subordination. Whatever life-expressing form we keep in mind, characteristic of it will be an interpenetrating of all psychic functions. In a great work of art the inner and outer world are linked together, the gap between subjective organization and objective environment is narrowed down; man reveals himself as capable of assimilating the most dreadful experience by transforming it into melodious and rythmical sounds, harmonious colors or shapes, and architectonic thoughts, which, in turn, make the impact of the outer world less intense, and our impulses and conations more adaptive.

Our psychic life is not a chaos of isolated contents. It shows a certain order, structure. In the creative man they are more apparent and find a wider and richer realization. But there is already genuine creativeness in our elementary functions. Sensations are never given as such, but rather as apperceptions. This transformation is spontaneous, a fact which has led us to assume that the conception of the whole is characteristic of all our psychic life.

"In all living organisms there is a reaction to stimuli and a spontaneous activity which are not separated."[82] This activity is a continuous process of assimilation and selection. The selective force in us is a biological necessity. Of the innumerable sensations, only those become apperceptions which indicate and guide our needs. Our past would handicap us immensely if it were not for our ability to choose between experiences which further us and those which retard us. Indeed, our life would be an unending tragedy if it were not for our capacity to dispense with the thought of all the evils life has in store for us. We know that some day our body will decay; and yet we go on as if this process were of no concern to us. Our interests and passions for noble ideals could hardly persist if we were distraced by the many obstacles and pitiless forces of destruction. In the long run, no human being is spared the countless evils life involves. Bereavement, catastrophic changes of fortune, shocking disappointments in social relations, vicissitudes in love, are dread experiences for everyone. It is a matter of our creative faculties whether we assimilate them or not.

We respond to the impact of the outer world in different ways according to our constructive abilities. Our response can be poor or rich, narrow or wide, sheer imitation of standardized adjustments or an aspiration to new ones. We can be driven by impulses and implanted habits or by reflective consciousness, which is our strongest weapon in a world of ever changing conditions. Standardized forms quite often disguise disorganization,[83] and to follow them blindly means to perpetuate evil, errors fashioned to truths, and vices remade into virtues. As in the life of a single individual there may lurk real chaos behind a disguised integration, so in a society which sticks to old beliefs and tendencies, and ferrets out all kinds of reason to defend its shortcomings. We become creators wherever and whenever we discover such insufficiencies. Our will to self-expression is the driving force in overcoming obstacles.[84] With deep penetration into intrinsic forces of life, with the grasping of its limitations and opportunities, its hazardous and constant elements, grows an unrest, a tension, and where there is tension there too, is a tendency to surmount it. Alexander speaks of the passionate excitement, "a feeling of unrest which keeps one in suspense, but a directed suspense like that we are aware of when we try to remember a name which we have forgotten, but know that it is connected with this, that and the other circumstance, and we feel ourselves straining towards it but unattaining. Over and above this, the impulse is felt mainly in bodily repercussions, in the visceral organs of secretion, about the heart and down back and all over the body. It is a directed restlessness, for it varies according to the topic, but what it is the indication of, what hidden movings urge us forward into the customary outlet of words or other forms of artistic material, is not disclosed until we have in semi-blindness achieved the desired product."[85] Nietzsche thinks of creation as salvation, liberation from suffering. Our will plays the most important role in it. "To will," says Nietzsche, "is to create."[86] In its result creation is pleasure, in its beginning, pain.[87] To pierce the depth of life does not require experiencing much. It is enough, says Guyau, to have suffered intensely.[88] There is a wide gap between man and man, conditioned by inherited and developed potentialities, depth and range of experiences. The narrow self which seldom surpasses mere bodily demands never becomes creative. In order to create we must enlarge our self, make it a resonance of a wider, social self. To penetrate reality, to dwell in its entanglements means to reveal, to discover. Each discovery conveys knowledge. By getting to know ourselves and nature we become alert to dangers and awake to new opportunities. To find a problem is to invoke the feeling of tension, unrest; to solve a problem means to stir the most intense and enduring pleasure, especially when this solution turns out to be a blessing for humanity. Will to self-expression becomes creative when it is permeated with a passionate love for mankind.

Man creates as a social being. To share experiences with other fellow men is a great enjoyment which is enhanced by the number of those we carry communion with. The most dreadful experience becomes bearable when we find a response in other people. To express it, to convey it, is to find an outlet for a necessary psychocatharsis. To express it in appropriate form is to make it material for our creative abilities. Whether we are among people or in seclusion pondering some problem, we are holding communion with other people, of the present and past. After all, creations of the past—paintings, sculptures, poems, philosophies—are lively social stimuli to which we react. We create as a part of a larger group, whether we accept its norms and values or we fight against them. In both cases there is interaction and interpenetration.[89] The new trend a creator calls into being may be a result of steady controversy with the current movement. Let us just think of Schopenhauer and Nietzsche. Both elaborate their thoughts in conscious opposition to prevalent philosophies and social trends of their time. In the case of Schopenhauer it was the metaphysical idealism of Hegel which led to his "World As Will And Idea." In the case of Nietzsche it was the materialism of Strauss and the political smugness and complacency of his time which led to opposition. The more sensitive a creator is, the better equipped is he to grasp current trends. The response may be positive or negative. He may gather all given fragmentary values in a more integrated whole, or, driven by an indomitable will to reform, he may be animated by an ideal whose realization falls into a distant future.

Man does not create "in the void, culture establishes the background, furnishes the reasons back of creation . . ."[90] The fulfillment of his constructive abilities is conditioned by external circumstances, possibilities and opportunities relative to time and people. Favorable environment, pro-

74

pitious economic and political conditions enhance creative activities, call into life new expressive forms. Any sign of man's creation, given in an objective form, reveals his life. Primitive expressive forms indicate a primitive life. The richer our life becomes the more eloquent and significant its forms. An ever expanding life begets steadily new modes of expression.

To create means to give to some part of our life a physical embodiment, in words, colors, tones, etc.. This life is not fixed, ready-made, but grows and undergoes transformations in the creative process. Alexander refutes Croce's theory according to which creation is supposed to be a mere translation of a given mental state.[91] The artist does not translate into the material the images he has already in his mind. He proceeds "by stages, filling up his general impression into fullness."[92] The images the artist has in his mind at the beginning of his work and at the end are not the same. The first ones are obscure, more or less "vague, unconscious stirrings." The images of the artistic product are lively and clear concepts, appropriate through and through to the referred content. We do not know in advance all activities of our psychic life until the work is finished. In the creative process itself we grow, our self is being enlarged in all those acts of transcendence of our mind in different fields. For us who experience a created work as for the creator himself, his product is a discovery, a revelation of his life in a well integrated form.[93]

The creative process goes on as a steady flow of psychic contents which in order to become embodied in material form must show a certain order, interrelation, coordination, subordination, balance and proportion. These psychic contents consist of conscious and unconscious elements. The term of the unconscious goes back to Leibnitz who speaks about unclear psychic movements (which he calls perceptions, distinguished from apperceptions as clear, definite conscious elements). Nietzsche calls our consciousness a mere accident in the larger psychic life. For Goethe creation has its roots in the unconscious. Freud ascribes to the unconscious all repressed experiences from our early childhood. Jung gives us a wider definition of the unconscious. According to him, in all our images there is a part of human psychology, human destinies, joys and sorrows, likes and dislikes. Beliefs and tendencies experienced by our ancestors are experienced by ourselves in our unconscious. "Our most effective ideals are variations of some archetype."[94] Nietzsche speaks of two creative forces in us: Dionysian and Apollonian. The first represents the chaotic emotional life, the second the ordered conceptual and imaginative life. The Dionysian principle describes our impersonal urge to transcend and overflow the self; the Apollonian force is the more personal, contemplative ability to assimilate our most dreadful experience in delightful, enchanting images.

There is a close connection between the unconscious and inspiration. Lange gives us a very good explanation of inspiration. Suppose we try very hard, day after day, to solve a problem. We become nervous, we feel a tension. Over and over again prejudices, errors, detours prevent us from proper solution. All these cumbersome endeavors and preliminary trials may be forgotten. Then, suddenly we find a solution and are overwhelmed by a feeling of relief. The tension ceases, and we are overcome by a passivity as if this solution had been instilled in us by some external power.[95] Inspiration, in a wider sense, is the name for immediate, intuitive grasping of relations and correlations without the arduous work of inference. Many of our activities are performed in this way as soon as we achieve perfection in some field. What turns out to be inspiration, intuition for the expert, requires deductive and inductive steps on the part of the layman. The spontaneity of some of our insights is not spontaneous at all when we take into consideration all previous trials and various unconscious elements. They are spontaneous in becoming conscious. The passive emotional response resulting from such intuitive graspings leads to objectivation and projection. Many a creator speaks of himself as an instrument of a higher power.[96] This inclination to hypostatize is a residue of our archaic thinking, which substantiates and objectifies spiritual processes.

In the process of creation our whole psychic life grows, and this activity is a source of intense, enduring pleasure. Creative function is free of the innumerable distractions of daily life. It is harmonious, it has tension, suspense and relief. Groos compares creating to playing.[97] In both there is enjoyment resulting from the functioning of the organs, actualizing of abilities, pleasure in experimenting, a conscious deceiving and discarding of highly affective life. Groos disregards the deeper meaning of creation, its social import. Let us just think of the many sacrifices which great works of art require. Cases where men neglected their health are legion. Their persistent and strong-will effort has its roots in the belief that by their deeds the common good of mankind has been augmented.

Impulses to creation are manifold: the urge to form, to effective discarding, to reveal, to confess, to commune, the will to self-assertion, pride, vanity, fame, sympathy toward fellow-men, eros, sex and its ramifications.[98] They all can be traced down to the genuine urge to self-expression and self-expansion which is a social urge. Only as a part of a social self does man aspire to perfect expressions. To give life form, enduring, shareable and communicable form, means to preserve this life from generation to generation. Great men are driven by the desire to perpetuate themselves in an extremely individual way, as spiritual beings. They reach their goal when the uniqueness of their life finds a unique form. The impulse to creation is not a sublimated libido spur (Freud). New discoveries have disclosed that even men of few inhibitions create, and poverty of expressive forms is not related to lack of sexual repressions. Our creativeness stands in direct proportion to our knowledge. The deeper we penetrate reality, the more we know, the more abundant become our expressive forms. Were values nothing but sublimated libido energies, they could not, in return, influence the libido itself, which they in fact do. Who can deny that our sexual passion increases when the desired object becomes an expression of values? Vitality and creativeness do not stand in reverse relation.

Our "actual world is a combination of movement and culmination, breaks and reunion,"[99] of chaos and order, fragments and totalities; and this polarity enables us to create values which are, to a certain extent, arrested moments of our life. There is no absolute gap between reality and values. After all, what we call reality is nothing but the world perceived and comprehended by us. Our concepts about the universe have a history just as have our ideas of beauty and goodness. Whoever talks about absolute, ultimate values denies their dynamic character. Since they are results of, and directing factors in, the interaction between our organization and physical and social events, they are in a state of constant becoming because we and our environment change too. With the development of our senses we learn to see better and penetrate deeper. With the evolution of our emotions and cognitions our responses turn out to be richer, more adequate. To make expressive forms of life final, means to cut off progress. History is full of examples of that which was once reason and blessing becoming nonsense and a curse. If a society tries, by all its means, to live up to values which were called into life by different circumstances, such a society sooner or later dooms itself.

Man not only creates values, and in so doing gives expression to his life, but values given in different objects condition his life to a wide degree. Under the impact of values man develops his constructive abilities to the utmost, actualizes his aim with vigor and persistency, toils and accepts every sacrifice until his work is finished. Were values nothing more than mere ejaculations, evinced feelings, they could never induce man to do the arduous work which creation means. We could not serve truth were truth not one of the living forms of humanity itself, manifesting the dignity of man as a reflective social being. Values express his urge to transcend his craving for order and harmony, for higher accomplishments than those ever attained. The relativity of values is rooted in life itself, which, from the spiritual point of view, is a steady transition. The fact that the truth of one generation turns into error for another, certainty into probability, belief into superstition, right into wrong, speaks for the reality of values as life expressions. An ever-expanding life calls for transvaluations.

With his creations man gives meaning to life, raises it to a higher level and in actualizing his potentialities, makes it into the material of his molding forces. There are no limitations or finalities in this his doing. Brute existence itself imposes on him problems of the most complicated character. We may ponder upon sickness, death, evils of nature and evils of men day and night, but are never content in submitting to these facts. Our fear, uncertainty, consciousness of our insignificance in the immense universe, may be alleviated from time to time with some happy thought, vision, or lofty emotion, but will recur, again and again. No matter how much we may indulge in such pessimistic meditations, we cannot help but admit that life expressed and transformed by values becomes the most intense stimulant. Values have a highly social function. They propagate understanding and moral communion, bind us together, and by invoking common sensations, emotions and cognitions make us feel as members of a greater whole. They liberate us from depressing isolation. By participating in values we do not feel strangers in a world driven by fear and despair. Still better integrated is the creator himself. He feels secure, has his feet on the solid ground, and is overwhelmed by a divine calmness. In such a state he will speak of the world *sub specie aeternitatis* and he will dream of an infinite spirit unifying all of us in a better and more dignified life.

It is characteristic of great spiritual works that they offer satisfactions and stir new dissatisfactions. Whoever makes science or art the aim of his life, will sooner or later add to the existing values some new ones. To understand values means, at the same time, to experience the push forward they imply. True experiences are not only intakings but also outgivings. Any advance is surmounting of obstacles. If it were not for values, we could never conceive of those innumerable shortcomings and insufficiencies which stir us to create. Life reflected by values becomes a steppingstone, a bridge to higher forms. It is true, man likes to deceive himself. He takes his wishes for realities, he likes to dream a better world where all struggle ceases, and he confuses his dream with existence. But he himself wakens up to his dreams. The world is changeable, in a steady flux, so he anticipates an intelligible realm of perfection and absoluteness. But he himself later on dismisses this edifice as an illusion. Whole philosophical systems are thus built and destroyed. His will to truth may be obscured for a certain time, but in the long run it comes back to life, more vigorous, more energetic. Were it not for the vitality of our mind, we would still dream the dream of our ancestors, the world of magic, myths, nymphs and demons.

All progress is the result of a true discovery, of revealing reality in all its complexities. We become creative when we learn to see and penetrate deeper. As in our daily life we do not assimilate hard experiences by closing our eyes to them, but by their full comprehension, so the great man has to dwell in the intrinsicalities of life in order to integrate it. The better adjusted he himself becomes, the more perfect turns out his creation.

Each step forward is the fruit of a full realization of all these norms, standards, beliefs and tendencies which become lifeless, disguised expressions of disorder. Changes in environment, social and economic shiftings, call for new adaptations, new values.

Each achievement is the result of a struggle against the inertia which binds us to obsolete forms, old ties and fashions fallacies to truths in all kinds of pseudoscientific terms. Applause and pleasure are not indicative of values when they appeal to our vile, selfish passions and flatter us rather than stir our dissatisfactions to the utmost. It is the invoked longing, craving for something higher, which true values aspire to.

Each push forward is a push forward of all values. No beauty will thrive in a sphere of moral chaos, no morality will develop where no sense of beauty exists and where economic needs burden us and absorb most of our time. Religious values can only expand in harmony with others. Knowledge is the vital source of all values. A better known subject matter always calls for more appropriate expressive forms.

CHAPTER IV

Aesthetic Values

Created beauty, embodied in different forms, reveals
and stimulates the activity of our mind. The degree of
beauty or its perfection stands in direct proportion to this
activity. Beauty which stirs our senses only is a lower
value than beauty which arouses and enhances our whole
psychic life, our emotions, conations and cognitions, in an
harmonious, integrated way.[100] Our sensual data are only
the first step in the experience of aesthetic values. Whoever narrows down beauty to immediately given impres-
sions, overlooks the complexity of mental activities which
find an embodiment in the creative process, and which are
characteristic of our aesthetic experience.[101] The aesthetic
object reveals itself "only after a process of activity and
a series of physical and mental adjustments."[102] Mere
passive submission to the object does not effect the grasping of its value. "Without an act of recreation the object
is not perceived as a work of art. The artist selects, sim-
plifies, clarifies, abridges and condenses according to his
interest. The beholder must go through these operations
according to his point of view and interest. In both, an
act of abstraction, that is, of extraction of what is significant, takes place. In both, there is comprehension in its

83

literal signification — that is, a gathering together of details and particulars physically scattered into an experienced whole. There is work done on the part of the percipient as there is on the part of the artist."[103] "The work of art throws the spectator back into the frame of mind in which the artist produced it."[104] Aesthetic appreciation has different degrees of adequacy, the highest when it comes close to aesthetic creation. Without abilities, congenial with those of the artist himself, we grasp only fragments of his creation. Our aesthetic sense has to be trained, cultivated, to encompass all the richness which a perfect work of art harbors. Furthermore, we must be driven by the same passion for the represented subject matter, for the problem which it involves, and must feel with the creator the same tension any deep penetration into events invokes. To enjoy a discovery, a revelation, in that appropriate form which art aims at, we must grasp the social function of the aesthetic values. Real art does more than entertain. It sustains and enhances the enduring feeling of belonging together. Our common joys and sorrows, common hopes and fears, common frailty and strength find here an expression which, when fully comprehended, calls for a deep sympathy towards mankind. Any shareable and communicable expression of a great life points to better adjustments and harmonious integration of our will with the will of others. It binds us by virtue of its vital communion not limited by space and time. It is not enough to feel art in order to comprehend its social importance. Any true appreciation is bound up with an intellectual process, a reflective consciousness.[105] When we learn to look at art as rational beings, and do not content ourselves with sensual and emotional responses, we become better equipped to discern values from dis-values, beauty from ugliness. It is the range and depth of the penetrated subject matter and its formal appropriate-ness which decide upon a work of art. To reveal a subject in all its essential qualities means to increase our knowl-edge, and by knowing things and ourselves we find ways of better adjustments. It is the ultimate goal of all creations, to help man make his world a more inspiring stimulus by realizing that in his social expansion lies his fulfillment. Truth combines us, knits bonds of mutual understanding, and keeps those emotions and conations alive which ef-fect a self-expansion. A socialized self is rich, strong, knows no fear and despair of loneliness, nor the un-bearable sadness of a life devoid of any aim, which is indicative of an inert, selfish individual. Error separates us, feeds our prejudices, excites blind passions of hatred and aggressiveness, which finally lead to self-destruction. Beauty and ugliness are in this respect related to truth and error. Beauty widens our world, ugliness narrows it; beauty begets love, ugliness hatred; beauty appeals to con-structive abilities, ugliness breeds annihilating, devastating impulses. Whether a work of art belongs to beauty or ugliness depends upon its true, real or false, unreal subject matter and its adequate or inadequate form. No matter how skillful an artist may be, his work will not attain per-fection if he has not the gift of a great seer and is not able to find behind his personal-all-too-personal needs and gratifications, joys and sorrows, human-all-too-human ex-periences. His psychocatharsis, ensuing in the creative process, becomes a human psychocatharsis when he has the power to surmount his narrow horizon in all these acts of transcendence which his work requires. Only in this case will his work "excel his personal fate."[106] Without the passion for the revealed subject and the urge to effect a better society by disclosing actualities and pointing to ideal potentialities a great work of art has never been created.

Aesthetic values can be low or high, poor or rich, narrow or wide, small or large. They differ in greatness. What is aesthetic greatness? It depends upon the largeness of the subject matter and appropriateness of form. In this regard beauty can be compared to goodness and truth. The degrees of goodness are degrees of its magnitude. "A good savage is as good as a good Christian, but his goodness is not so large, because it is appropriate to simpler conditions."[107] With truth it is the same. "The man of science has attained the scientific end if he has discovered a property of a species of plants as much as if he has discovered the formula of the law of gravitation. But the two truths are not comparable in greatness."[108]

Aesthetic perfection is not a matter of form alone, nor of content alone, but of both. The larger the subject matter the more complicated becomes the task of expressing it in adequate form. Men of small caliber dwell in trifling subjects, and insignificant subjects, no matter how skillfully represented, invoke transient responses, emotional thrills. Great men choose larger, profounder themes, whose tackling calls for unique, unsurpassable abilities. The greatness we confer upon them is our admiration, our tribute for the aroused psychic activities, for the enduring impression.

Perfect beauty is a harmonious fusion of form and subject matter, which fusion enables us to recreate represented life. In this way arrested moments regain their life continuum. (Do we admire Rembrandt's "Portrait Of An Old Woman" merely on account of its richness of color, its technical achievement? It is the artist's grasp of age in its full dynamics which makes this painting a unique one.) To express life means conquering its fragmentary, chaotic, disorganized elements and bringing them into coherence, consistency, order. Art could never play an important part in our life if life itself did not contain some rudimentary forms of order, coherence. The fact that beauty gratifies our senses, elates our emotions, enlightens our cognitions and helps us to better integration, speaks for a certain affinity between reality and value.

Beauty is more than unity in variety, proportion, balance, symmetry, rhythm. It is life-informing, life-furthering and life-perpetuating by means of physical embodiments. To lift the latter to aesthetic objects means to impute life to them. This imputing is our active response,[109] which is not an arbitrary process, depending upon our moods, or our current emotional and cognitive state. Our response is invoked and guided by the aesthetic object. The richer and more significant the represented subject matter, the more vital its dynamic form, the intenser our activity will be, provided we approach the aesthetic object with congenial faculties. If our senses are not sufficiently trained, if our intellect is not properly developed, we will never grasp the aesthetic value behind its physical embodiment. Beauty is not an immediately given quality, like color, which we perceive. It is real by virtue of the psychic dynamic, it objectifies and communicates. In order to do this the object must conform to certain conditions, norms, which vary with the material of art and the represented subject. This conformity speaks against any relativism and subjectivism (subject thought of as individual, and not as species man) of aesthetic values. To know what art is aiming at, to know its actual limitations and ideal potentialities, helps a great deal in our experience and appreciation of values. Much confusion in our valuative judgments comes from ignorance. When from a composition we expect the same that a poem offers, when from a picture we await that which a play can give us, when we assume a created work of art to be a mere acquiescence in our wants, illusions and wishes, sooner or later we shall turn aesthetic subjectivists and deny any objectivity of values. Any revelation conveys some knowledge. The adequate response to knowledge is not liking or disliking, but comprehension. As there are truths which please and truths which do not please, so there are aesthetic values which arouse intense pleasure and aesthetic values which waken us from self-complacency and stir our dissatisfactions with given situations. They are living reminders of our weakness, our inertia, our injustice, our chaos disguised in all kinds of false ideals. To expect from art the mere disclosing of "beautiful" things, comes close to cutting its life nerve. No great artist, no great poet will consent to being an exponent of prevailing beliefs and tendencies when these implant and perpetuate human misery, social barriers, caste prejudices. Great artists will expose man's shame with the same vigor and eloquence with which they espouse man's glory.[110]

Objectivity Of Aesthetic Values.

The objectivity of aesthetic values is bound up with thir shareable and communicable character.[111] This fact does not suggest that all men must experience beauty in the same way or react to it with the same psychic dynamic. We know what training in physics it requires to grasp some fundamental truths. With aesthetic values it is not different. We have to cultivate our senses to apprehend all intricate qualities a picture or symphony contains. We must train our intellect to follow the poet or writer through his discoveries. Our response to beauty may be reduced to inarticulate feelings if we are not well equipped to recreate its life. Furthermore, we may be hampered by transmitted values, blindly accepted without reflection. The events of the past, social structure, taboos and inherited beliefs leave their stamp on our conception of beauty,[112] and it takes long critical education to overcome all these impeding influences. As in grasping scientific discoveries, so too, in experience of aesthetic creations a standard mind is prerequisite.[113] Standard mind is not something mysterious, nor a property of a few outstanding individuals. We all contribute to it in the arduous way we cultivate our senses and cognitive abilities. We must live in science in order to keep step with its steady advance. We must live in aesthetic values to keep ourselves abreast of their transformations. Life on its spiritual level expands, and with its growth our value standard changes, becomes richer, wider, better qualified to discern true values from pseudo-values. That so many average works of art find immediate appeal, while perfect achievements wait for recognition, does not speak for subjectivism and relativism of their value, but rather for the retrogressive and obscurant tendencies of those who evaluate.

Objectivity of values does not mean their absoluteness. We do not have finalities in science, still less can we expect ultimateness in art. All values are relative to time and people, to circumstances, to all those opportunities which further man's creativeness. We change, and with that goes a transformation of our values which is indicative of our attitudes, likes and dislikes, our mental and moral state, our ignominy and dignity, our actual attainments and distant possibilities. Spiritual life expands, "in expressing itself in matter."[114] Its objectified forms sustain and enliven our creative consciousness. Today we may discard Hegel's idealism as a speculative metaphysical quest, but in one thing we can still agree with him: that a reflective consciousness is a vital source and most effective guidance in our physical adaptation and social adjustment. We move on the same level with the savage as long as we are driven by blind passions, beliefs and tendencies devoid of reason. All progress is a transition from irrational reactions to rational responses. Creative intelligence does not tame or subdue our vital impulses, but directs them to a complete fulfillment. Reasonableness is not opposed to our emotions and conations; it is a "quality of an effective relationship" among them.[115]

Beauty Is Not An "Intrinsic" Value.

Created beauty reveals through sensuous media some part of our life. To grasp its value means to recreate this life, to make it our own. All of us can express joys and sorrows, hopes and fears, but only the great artist has the gift of making this expression a finished, consummate one. By doing so he conquers chaotic, inchoate and fragmentary elements and gives meaning to the most accidental phenomena. In our daily life we are seldom diverted from all-too-practical interests. Weighted down by the dullness of routine work, we turn into passive automata, rather driven by, than directing, the impacts of our environment. Artistic expression bestows upon us the calmness of a rapt experience. Our admiration is heightened because we know what effort, what exertion precedes a perfect work of art, because we envision the chaos the creator had to conquer, the pains he had to endure, to transform something amorphous into an enchanting, captivating shape. The most dreadful experience affects us aesthetically because the artist, by giving it an appropriate form, manifests his command over it. To control an experience means to assimilate it, and each assimilation is a kind of surmounting. The perfect fusion of form and content which is indicative of beauty points to the effected transformation of the experience. Here we find nothing indifferent, irrelevant. The most fortuitous element turns significant. We speak of consistency, coherence, unity in variety, balance, proportion, as objective constituents of beauty; but form receives its aesthetic quality through the subject matter it reveals, informs and perpetuates. Created beauty is representative.[116]

Beauty is not an intrinsic value, it is not appraised as an end in itself. Values in their objectified forms are physical embodiments of our life, and, as such, serve to perpetuate this life. They not only depict actualities but also ideal potentialities. As individual expressions of particular integrations they stir emulating impulses in many. Spiritual values (beauty is a form of these) are higher than economic because they engender and further the transition of our narrow, bodily self, and effect its emergence into a larger, richer, social self. Beauty has a highly social function. True art helps us to comprehend our common nature, and this understanding leads to a common reaction toward mankind. With the revealing and communicating of the subject matter goes the effort to unite us with it. We speak of art as "sympathetic representation."[117] A sympathetic representation leads to a sympathetic response. The expressed life becomes our own, and since it bears the stamp of its creator, we grow with him, his adjustment becomes ours. A deep steeping in the formed subject transforms ourselves. Our particular ephemeral aims give place to a nobler end, which is a more dignified humanity. Beauty makes us malleable to the requirements of social life.

Kant is wrong when he defines beauty as "purposiveness without purpose," and traces it down to the constructive impulse, which, diverted from practice, becomes contemplative.[118] Man behaves as a unit and cannot be divided in an acting and contemplating being. To make us forget practical needs is not what true art aspires to. It does not cause us to become dreamers of illusory worlds, but helps us to face reality in a more auspicious and consonant way, aids us to remake the evils caused by men in their ignorance. It is not passivity which it acclaims, but enhanced activity. When art turns out to be a refuge and escape, it accomplishes just the opposite of what it intends. We return from this temporary seclusion with more bitterness and greater despair, with hate instead of love.

Aesthetic values thrive only where economic and social conditions are salutary, advantageous, where man's misery is reduced to a minimum. We cannot make man realize the blessings of art when the daily struggle for the most primitive needs weighs upon him. Beauty is not a substitute for food, nor a suitable remedy for discomfort, want and destitution. Great artists have never been content with applauding prevailing conditions. "The first stirrings of dissatisfaction and the first intimations of a better future are always found in art."[119]

Beauty And Pleasure.

We speak of perceptions, emotions, conations and cognitions as if they were discrete units, clearly distinguishable from each other. In reality they are interwoven phases of a dynamic process. Whoever speaks of the exclusive emotional response to beauty, of the exclusive will response to goodness, of the exclusive cognitive response to truth, is still influenced by a psychology which used to accept uncritically the mechanistic character of our life, a psychology which tried to imitate the classic physics of Newton. Modern science has replaced the mechanistic universe by the dynamic world-outlook. The realm of matter has turned out to be a world of energy. Molecules, atoms changed from simple parts to the most complex configurations. Organization, interrelation of parts, transformation of energies, are no less indicative of psychic life. Here we find no elements, but smaller or larger contexts, not static entities, phenomena, but functions differently organized; not accidental occurrences, but purposive actions. Mind becomes a term for the psychic dynamic which can only be treated and comprehended in its wider context with the physical environment. This, and our own organization condition each other, and the steady interaction makes life a continuous transition. The creative process is the most energetic form of such transformations; it reveals our mind in its enhanced activity. Aesthetic values denote this activity.

When we analyze the concept of beauty and trace it down to its constituent factors we find: that created beauty is given in some physical embodiment, sounds, ilnes, colors, etc.. This material figures as a medium of expression. In order to become an aesthetic object this material must be arranged in such a way as to appear charged with life, meaning. Such objectified forms are projected moments of our life. Perceptual data are the starting point in experience of beauty. The better our senses are trained, the better qualified they will be to grasp all these fine color shapes and harmonies which beauty consists of. Since we enter "no situation mentally pristine,"[120] our perceptual data will differ widely. This diversity can be gradually reduced through a thorough training of our senses in the various aesthetic fields.

Perceptual data always have an emotional tonic; they please or displease. The greater the aesthetic value, the more intense our emotional response. Pleasure invoked by a mere stirring of our senses is weak and transient. Pleasure invoked by arousing our higher functions is intense and enduring. Beauty appeals to our conations too. As sympathetic representation of some part of our life, it excites and stimulates our will and conditions its motives. Our experience of beauty becomes complete with the aesthetic judgment. This, in turn, calls for comparison. In order to compare, we must know what art aims at; we must apprehend its limitations and possibilities. Even in music, the most abstract art, knowledge enhances experience to a tremendous degree. The final step in experience of beauty, like all other values, is the reflective consciousness. To reflect does not mean to analyze the whole in terms of its parts, it does not mean to belittle, to disparage. To reflect here means to find in the unique discovery of a certain aesthetic creation a pregnant value for mankind. We may indulge in aesthetic values day and night and still remain on their surface, so long as we do not comprehend their deeper mission, their social significance. Great men do not go through all the pains and sacrifices which creation requires just to please our senses, to appeal to our likes, to flatter our shortcomings. They are driven by the indomitable will to help mankind to a more dignified life.

Beauty And Ugliness.

Man is chaotic and organized, integrated; inert and

active; and because he is both, he may sink to the lowest level or rise to the highest glory. He may be driven by blind passions or noble ideals, and may find his vocation either in gratification of mere animal desires or in the fulfilment of his spiritual potentialities. This polarity finds an expression in his preferences, in all that he cherishes, craves, loves, hates. He will live in disvalues when chaos prevails in him; he will dwell in values when order becomes the predominant factor of his life. Values express and further our creative abilities; disvalues disclose and foster our destructive impulses.

Chaos is disintegration; it widens the gulf between our will and the will of others, and leads to isolation. Our self, devoid of all social bonds, turns against itself, becomes insane. Order is integration, coherence, consistency. It unites us, and this social emergence becomes the most adequate way for our self-maintaining. Chaos breeds ugliness, evil and wickedness; order begets beauty, goodness and holiness. Any push forward of humanity proceeds as a conquering of the chaotic elements in our nature. Whoever speaks of progress as a transcendent law, as a cosmic design which actualizes itself, step by step, independently of our endeavors, endangers any development which is a result of our will and intelligence. No less dangerous is a cynical attitude which sees in all order a mere deception, and assumes "an unchangeable human nature." The reality of our spiritual values is the best defense against such an unjustified pessimistic view. We could not create values, still less respond to them, if they were not realities of our life itself.

It is not curiosity which leads man to science, nor the

constructive urge which drives him to art.[121] Something much deeper does it, namely, the necessity of life itself, the transition from chaos to order, the Promethean will to form one's own life, the impetus "to gather the world" into one's mind "in a continuous activity that is harmonious and yet ever new."[122] Values are expressions of this activity, living symbols of what we are and what we aspire to. They are not artificial products added to life as something entirely incongruent with it, but forms of life itself, which undergoes steady changes, from simplicity to complexity, from bodily sustenance to spiritual expansion, from emotional reactions to reasonable responses, from vague social stirrings to moral acts, from superstition and ignorance to the inquiring reflective consciousness.

To say that value is what satisfies our desires, is to narrow down our life to passions and wants and to assume that they are static. Desires connote only one psychic function among others, and they change. They are determined by given circumstances, and by all the spiritual influences which values exert. Beauty not only satisfies actual conations but is also able to transform them, and to invoke new, more elated volitions.

To say value is identical with the pleasure an aesthetic object effects is to confuse an epiphenomenon of value experience, with value itself. Pleasantness results from the harmonious and intensified activity which creation and experience of values bring forth. Beauty is not a will quietive (Schopenhauer), but rather its vital stimulant and inducement.[123] Even in our deepest despair art turns out to be an exuberant solace. There are many reasons for this. Art sustains and promotes our creative abilities; it transforms the most dreadful experiences into an integrated psychic phenomenon; it satisfies our craving for order and wakens us to ideal possibilities of remaking the adversities and afflictions of life. By virtue of aesthetic values our interests are enlarged, our aims, although relative and finite in actuality, become infinite in their ideal potentialities. When we comprehend that our self finds its most adequate fulfilment in all the intakings and outgivings which a social life claims, we will not miss any opportunity to work in this direction. The reward is tremendous. We always have something to strive for; our problems gain in magnitude, making every solution a starting point for a new problem. We are spared that life-killing sadness which loneliness brings. To live in a social sphere means to grasp the continuity of our spiritual life. A selfish world is not only ugly, immoral, but a source of most intense pain. In our asocial seclusion we are tormented and plagued by the thought of death, whose sharp and frustrating pang decreases with our socializing. No matter how deeply we may ruminate and ponder upon death, our social self will find some cheering answer. It will point to the living tradition, to objectified spiritual values through which the human mind perpetuates itself. Fear of death increases with our asocial withdrawal, and decreases with our social emergence. To feel knit with our kind means to derive vital strength for ourselves. Where social life is crippled, reduced to a minimum, there we find the extreme forms of disorganization, disintegration, moral and intellectual derangements, infantile retrogressions which lead to crime and finally to self-extirpation.

The narrow, selfish individual is bound to make mistakes, detours. When we do not find the right outlet for our vital impulses, they weaken or turn into most destructive forces which break loose against our fellow men and ultimately against ourselves. Love changes to hatred, fury; compassion and forbearance to implacability and intolerance.

To assume that only values are genuine, real expressions of life and disvalues nothing but artificial products, is to indulge in naive optimism. No less naive is raven-black pessimism, which regards all culture as a factitious addition to nature, as hypostatized illusions, to cover the eternal beast in man. The optimist considers disvalues as nonexistent or very low values; the pessimist thinks of values as mitigated disvalues. The whole controversy is fruitless, devoid of facts. We need not meditate to make up our mind about Leibnitz or Schopenhauer. Both are wrong. They separate what is not separable. Man is creative and inert; and because he is both, he is moral and immoral, righteous and wicked. Values and disvalues are realities, neither of them mere deceptions. Our response to them is the best argument against every disjunction between value and existence. To speak of the cosmic congruence or incongruence of our values is preposterous and pretentious.

Man creates to better the human lot, to reduce the evils of nature and those perpetrated by men themselves. The former are great, but certainly not as multifarious as the latter. The number of victims of wars, and of religious and racial persecutions surpasses the total of victims of natural cataclysms. Unfortunately, the same material, which becomes the physical embodiment of a value, may turn into an expression of a disvalue. We have science, art, religion; we have pseudo-science too, pseudo-art and pseudo-religion. Our language serves them both. The choice between values and disvalues is not a free option; it is a vital necessity. Our response to both of them reflects how much is in us of organization, how much of chaos, how much of man and how much of beast. Our positive attitude to an error does not change it to truth; neither does our response to ugliness change it to beauty. It reveals only the degree of refinement of our senses and emotions, and the strength of our reflective consciousness.

As in science, so with a work of art, greatness is not relative to the number of people who are able to grasp its value. It is the magnitude of the subject matter, the depth of its penetration and the expressive perfection which are decisive. Art, like science, is not confined to certain subjects. Whatever concerns man can become its object. The kind of representation determines whether an artist gives physical embodiment to beauty or ugliness. Human misery, ignoble and tragic entanglements, frailty and strength, happiness and despair, youth and age, the bliss and anguish of love — they all become aesthetic beauty through the great artist who makes them communicable and shareable experiences. No matter how peerless his expressive faculty may be, if he is not driven by a deep sympathy toward mankind, his work will be very insignificant. Only a great personality creates great, outstanding works of art; and greatness, in the proper sense of the word, is a moral term, applied to individuals socially well integrated. Here we find the best of humanity incarnate, the ineluctable urge to truth, realization of which often requires enormous sacrifices, with complete disregard of comfort, health, and even life itself. Jesus Christ, Socrates, Giordano Bruno, Galileo Galilei, Johann Huss, victims of human stupidity and cruelty, will shine forever as eternal paragons. They are the best proof against hedonism, which thinks of man as a pleasure-seeking animal. Here we find virtues of splendor and magnitude actualizing in a continuous participation in human destiny; generosity and fairness towards fellow men, and not mere tolerance, the disguised form of infantile superiority; the will to espouse what is good and creative in man, and expose his shortcomings, his inertia which ties him to the beliefs of remote, barbaric ancestors.

Life as revealed by great artists always implies some ideal, prospective elements. Here lies the deep reason why works of art which deal with our tragical conflicts and evil forces, with calamities caused by nature and by men, leave an enduring impression, while others which are concentrated on the rosy side of life and comical situations evoke merely passing responses. The transient impression of a comedy and the lasting impression of a tragedy are explicable by many facts. Man is a prospective being; he wants better adjustments and integrations than those already realized. A great tragedy is the product of a profound penetration into human nature, and as such, discloses causes of human misery. By getting to know the causes we are better equipped to master them. Awareness of shortcomings is the first step toward improvement. Through the great passion of his hero, the poet stirs our symphaty too. The life of the hero becomes our own, and our highly agitated self thus becomes more alert to all the pitiless forces men turn loose against men. We grasp the beauty of tragedy when we comprehend the evil behind the misfortune that has befallen, a comprehension which animates us to fight the beast in man, ignorance, social injustice, aggressiveness, intolerance, tyranny.

Whenever we realize fully the destructiveness of disvalues, our response to values is enhanced, our will to preserve and perpetuate them strengthened. The unending misery begotten of ignorance, calls the blessing of knowledge to clearer consciousness. The derangement of an immoral life makes for a more adequate appreciation of our constructive, social impulses. Political slavery, tyranny, mass-murder committed because of religious prejudices, point in a most effective way to the worth of freedom.[124] It is not enough to cherish values whenever and wherever disvalues thrive. We must fight the latter with the same vigor which is necessary for preservation of values. Passive tolerance of crime is as bad as committing a crime. Pacifistic acquiescence in evil contributes to its growth. Such an attitude is not nobility, it is defeatism in its worst form.

Chapter V

MORAL VALUES

Could knowledge become a common good, and could our comprehending abilities be equally developed, we would not need laws to enforce moral acts. The choice between morality and immorality is a choice between self-preservation and self-extirpation and, no human being in full possession of his senses can hesitate as to which to choose. It is ignorance that makes him a supine prey and willful agent of all the destructive, chaotic impulses which are indicative of an immoral life. Moral insanity goes hand in hand with mental insanity. History has proven it on many occasions. All the tyrants, fanatics, enemies of human dignity, who heaped misery upon misery, were children of chaos. Their relentlessness and implacability were results of their paranoia, dementia. No less deranged were their millions of followers who put them on a pedestal. To worship brute force is always a sign of mental infantilism.

Immoral life is disintegrated, disorganized life. Its badness is as genuine as its ugliness, and not a mere interpretation. Were disvalues and values nothing but arbitrary explications of value-irrelevant facts, we could never find a way out of the consequent relativism and subjectivism. Value-irrelevant facts are non-existent and unknown to human beings. To act means to prefer, to select, to grasp the important and neglect the unimportant, to shift attention from one thing to another, to descend upon objects which descent makes them aimed, purposive, to narrow down the gap between ourselves and the environment in a continuous process of adaptation and integration. Valuing and valuation are deeply rooted in our life. They refer to values, not as transubjective entities hovering above us, but as efficacies of things and events, as dynamic forms of our life; they refer to our dispositions and the mode of their actualization, to the social patterns of intellectual and moral communion which find expression in the creative process.

No matter how sublime our ideas of beauty or goodness may be, they remain pale shadows so long as we think of them as absolute entities, independent of reality. Beauty in itself, goodness in itself, eternal, unchangeable, perfect paradigms—these are not human creations, and, as such, not life-furthering. With the assumption of eternal values goes hand in hand the conception of everlasting evil. Such metaphysical indulgings are very harmful. They take away from us all responsibility for our misdeeds and shortcomings and feed our inertia. Only if we make man understand that goodness is a vital necessity and the most propitious form of his life, can we, at the same time, animate him to fight evil, wherever he finds it, in himself and in others.

Behind metaphysical speculations is the artificial disjunction between value and reality which in turn calls for nihilism and skepticism. Every ethical skepticism is doomed to failure for the simple reason that it either denies obvious facts or misinterprets them. Our self-preservation is bound to the self-preservation of others. To assume that social ties are not genuine and real but fictitious and spurious, means to rate man below an animal, whose parental and gregarious impulse no skeptic can deny. In his struggle with nature for food and shelter man has found in his fellow men essential and great assets. His socializing is dictated by necessities of life itself. In social groups man learned to conquer fear and uncertainty and to employ his vital impulses for highly constructive designs. Self-preservation calls for self-expansion in the way of creation. Man does not create in a void or into a void. His abilities develop by traversing all the roads of his forerunners, and are conditioned by favorable trends and responses of his time. No social life thrives without moral values. As aspirations of a few they become a common good of others, first as prohibitive rules, blindly executed, and later on, when organically assimilated, as expressions of life itself.

The misinterpreted facts are: the history of moral values, their dynamic character, their being determined by external factors, their relevance to time and people, their lack of absoluteness and finality. All these facts, properly explained, do not speak for an ethical skepticism. Like beauty and truth, goodness has its history. The change is a transition from simple to complex forms called into life by higher needs and larger interests. New discoveries, deeper penetrations into things and events, into human nature, have a decisive influence on our life the transformations of which reflect on our values. When we realized that our planet was only a tiny body in the vast universe, our whole attitude underwent a change. Knowledge is not a mere intellectual affair; it stirs and directs our total life. Because of this the values of an epoch become obsolete in another. This fact justifies an ethical skepticism no more than the modification of fundamental concepts in physics would vindicate a skepticism in our natural sciences.

The history of morality, like the history of other values, shows its ups and downs, progressive and retarding trends. Within the same social group we find pioneers of humanity and its greatest enemies,—reason for abiding sadness but certainly not for an ethical nihilism. The validity of goodness does not become relative because of the millions of decadents who confuse values with disvalues. The same imbeciles and criminals will chatter about the relativity of truth and untruth, beauty and ugliness. Such insane, Machiavellian expediences punish themselves in the long run. Obscurantism, ignorance, prejudices, beliefs and tendencies of our barbarian ancestors, enforce the revival of a chaotic primitive life which was irrationalism in its worst, most destructive form. We cannot forbid the murdering of one group of people and sanction that of another. By doing so we take from murder its abhorred, repugnant quality. Besides, no concept can imply an affirmation and a negation at the same time. To expect us to consider murder, hate, lies, intolerance, aggressiveness, as both good and evil is to violate a fundamental principle of thinking, the principle of identity.

The existence of human society proves the reality of

moral conduct, and moral conduct attests the objectivity of moral values. To bring them to our reflective consciousness, to help us realize their propitious character in effecting a better adjustment and fulfillment of our creative abilities, that is the proper task of ethics. Such a task cannot be performed "beyond good and evil." Nietzsche would not have come to his "disvaluation" of values had he not forgotten that man is an acting being, and that his thinking has no other purpose than to guide him to a better and richer adjustment to the physical and social environment.

No human being acts beyond good and evil. His preferences may be implanted by tradition or may be the results of reasoning; they may have roots in blind passions or in elated emotions; they may reflect on his narrow or wide horizon; they may indicate a man of small caliber or a great personality. They will always reveal a set of values without which life would be impossible. From a man who writes treatises on morals we expect an elucidation of our moral values, and such a scientific interpretation can never be a relativism or a complete discarding of values. To be indifferent is not human and not even subhuman, as the life of animals shows. Nietzsche himself very soon abandoned his standpoint beyond good and evil. He divulged his love for the Antichrist, Cesare Borgia, the ruthless blonde beast, and became a worshipper of brute, cruel force. Had he considered those millions of victims of ruthless power, or himself as its possible prey, he could not have indulged in such harmful speculations, devoid of reason. Good and evil cannot be decided upon by cynical, haughty meditations. They have and will always be decided by life itself, because they imply the choice between its preservation and obliteration. The rise of "the slaves" against their "masters," the rise of Christ against Rome, was a rejuvenation of humanity, and not, as Nietzsche wants us to believe, its decline.

Moral And Immoral Acts.

Our behavior is motivated. There is no random motion in the life of an animal, still less so in our life. We share the determination of our actions with the animal, furthermore, fundamental physiological needs and a few primitive intellectual insights. Our advantage lies in the plasticity of our senses, in the flexibility of our impulses, in our unlimited ability to form habits, and, finally, in our intellect. All these assets can make a man a highly social being. Since we are born in a social environment our sociability is not an artificial product; it springs to life with our birth and develops constantly in the course of years. It is, no doubt, limited by hereditary potentialities; but these restrictions are small in comparison to the possibilities of a favorable environment. Modern research has disclosed that we have to be cautious in the enumerating of innate impulses. Their number is declining. We know that pugnacity is less inborn than acquired. There are primitive tribes which abhor aggressiveness. Besides, our drives and impulses, "although first in time, are never primary in fact."[125] In our behavior they are secondary; they depend upon interaction with a social medium.[126] The expressive forms of our impulses depend "upon the outlets and inhibitions supplied by the social environment."[127] "Any impulse may become organized into almost any disposition according to the way it interacts with surroundings. Fear may become organized into almost any disposition according to the way it interacts with surroundings. Fear may become abject cowardice, prudent caution, reverence for superiors, or respect for equals; an agency for credulous swallowing of absurd superstitions or for wary skepticism."[128] The various forms that our impulses may take in the course of their mutual interaction and their conditioning by a steadily changing environment are one of the most important fundaments of our moral life. The fact that the same vital impulse which exhibits destructiveness, can under other circumstances, display constructiveness, the fact that the same impulse which shows hatred, intolerance, may be transformed into love, fairness, are very encouraging findings which even the blackest pessimist cannot gloss over. Impulses, emotions, passions are strong or weak, intense or temperate. The kind of their outlet, the noble or ignoble end around which they cluster, make them moral or immoral.

The fault of any formalistic, rationalistic ethics lies not only in its method but in its goal too. We cannot effect a better moral life by casting the shadow of evil upon our passions and making them detestable. Life without passions, impulses, is empty, petrified. Our intellect is neither a master nor a servant of our impulses, but "their clarifier, liberator."[129] "Rationality . . . is the attainment of a working harmony among diverse desires . . . intelligence converts desire into plans, systematic plans based on assembling facts, reporting events as they happen, keeping tab on them and analyzing them."[130]

The intellect that guides our thoughts, guides our conduct. "Guide" is here used in a metaphorical sense. Intellect is not a static entity, different from our psychic functions. It is a name for the coherence and consistency of our thoughts, for the cooperation and integration of our impulses, emotions and conations. Intellectual efficiency is conditioned by our ability to acquire habits. "The essence of habits is an acquired predisposition to ways or modes of response, not to particular acts, except as under special conditions, they express a way of behaving. Habit means special sensitiveness or accessibility to certain classes of stimuli."[131] In a world of ever-changing conditions, circumstances, acquired habits without control of reason are insufficient implements. New situations call for new adjustments and new adjustments require new habits. The change of habits is effected by our intellect. It works by means of impulses, with habits as their prospective agent.

The noblest task of reason or intelligence is to attain a harmonious integration of our primary and secondary motivations. Primary are bodily needs and organic tensions; secondary are social determinants in the form of values. A blind discharge of vital impulses indicates a primordial, crude and barbarous life. Atrocious life is not only immoral, but undeveloped, poor, chaotic and disorganized and leads, in the long run, to self-annihilation. Freud speaks of the discomfort and uneasiness culture has brought about by restraining our passions.[132] Rather is the opposite true. Our vital impulses have found new constructive outlets through culture. Through his creations man achieved more comfort, conquered fear and uncertainty, alleviated his struggle for food and shelter, found means of controlling forces of nature and learned to avail himself of them. His cultural inhibitions became a tremendous asset. Out of them sprang a new life, a life of order and coherence, of beauty, a life where man stopped being a passive instrument of obscure "chance," where he realized his opportunities for taking fate into his own hands.

Morality stands and falls with our ability to bring the gratification of our vital needs and wants, into accord with the gratification of the needs of other people. This ability is a fact. We never respond "only to the immediate conditions of the present situation," but act "in accordance with biographical and social determinants of motivation that have long ago left their imprint."[133] Social patterns of behavior are operative factors in our wants and mode of their gratification, whether we are conscious of them or not. An absolutely asocial human being is not less fictitious than an absolute social one. "For even in relation to the satisfaction of tissue needs, different cultures will develop different practices which involve different kinds of accessory motivations."[134] The fusion of biological and social factors explains why each motivation "produces action in one direction and inhibits it in others."[135] Morality without inhibitions is non-existent; based exclusively on inhibitions, it leads to inactivity and becomes a lifeless phantom.

To become conscious of social determinants in our actions is the first step in our moral life. A blind, unreflected execution of moral norms makes our acts involuntary discharges, and may turn into a burden in an ever-shifting environment. The most important step in our morality is a critical, reflective attitude which varies with our knowledge. Right and well-founded knowledge leads to proper action. To comprehend the right and execute the wrong is a sign of disorganization. Social and moral maladjustments are not casual occurrences. Whenever and wherever they happen, we can trace them down to pathological symptoms of a mentally deranged personality. We can never become socially well integrated if chaos pervades our self. Inner incoherence, inconsistency, disharmony lead to incoherent, inconsistent, disharmonious acts.

We used to appraise moral and immoral acts according to their socially beneficial or detrimental results. Good and bad were terms applied to consequences of our behavior. With our deeper penetration into human nature, and following discoveries pertaining to the motivation process, good and bad became attributes of ourselves as the agents of moral and immoral acts. Moral acts are, in the proper sense of the word, voluntary. "A voluntary action is not a mere discharge of a feeling which is excited by the perception of an object, but it implies that the idea of the end to be attained is present not merely in consciousness, but to consciousness."[136] Deliberation and choice are its most essential characteristics. "Deliberation is a dramatic rehearsal (in imagination) of various competing possible lines of action ... it is an experiment in finding out what the various lines of possible actions are really like ..."[137] "Choice is not the emergence out of indifference. It is the emergence of a unified preference out of competing preferences."[138] To use reason in our choice does not mean to suppress our desires but to give them the most constructive outlet. To overlook in a present action the ensuing consequences is unreasonable. Such an attitude penalizes itself. Our volitions are aimed; they are directed toward ends. It is for our reason to deliberate on these ends, to find their furthering or retarding properties. We have near and distant goals. The realization of the latter requires thorough planning, persisting interests, and giving up immediate, transient pleasures in anticipation of a better and more enduring adjustment. In deliberating, reflecting upon, our ideas dwell in subsequent events of the course of action to be taken and do not go out to future pleasures, as the ethical hedonism erroneously assumes.[139]

Our "moral judgments are passed upon willed conduct or its equivalent, character."[140] Will, as substance, entity, power behind our volitions, is non-existent. Between a felt tension which precedes a conation and its execution there are many intermediary functions. The most important is the shifting of ideas. Due to it willed acts turn into a dynamic process.[141] Volitions are distinguished from each other by the nature of their objectives. Ends, aims motivate our actions when they are experienced as values. Our will-strength (in the metaphorical sense of this word) stands in direct proportion to impediments and obstructions which must be overcome, and to the large and inclusive objectives which call for long-range planning, persistency and endurance. From the ethical standpoint, will-strength is equivalent to the having and realizing of noble aims.[142]

113

Good And Bad.

"As there is no beauty till it is made through the artistic passion, neither are there rules of right and wrong till they are made through the slow but persistent push of the social instinct in its human form. Even elementary rules such as those of respect for human life, or of temperance are discovered through the wrath excited by the transgressor; as the stories of Cain and Noah illustrate. Concerned as these discoveries are with the simplest relations of life, they assume the character of invariable rules, for the impulses they reconcile are universal; and this identity in the solution of the great moral problems has often been mistaken for some peculiar and a priori even God-given character of moral laws."[143]

The historico-genetic approach to moral values reveals their functional significance. Little as we need metaphysical sanction for truth, no more do we need it for goodness. Besides, a metaphysical recourse involves the danger of making forms of life relative to time and people, to absolute, timeless expressions. Since good and bad are human creations, they can develop and undergo modification from inadequate to more appropriate forms of life. Such a transformation is a fact no scientific, unbiased, genetic approach can overlook. No doubt our aesthetic, moral and religious values may be traced to biological and utilitarian needs. We engrave all things and events in our memory, which gratify our desires, and in our gratitude we bestow upon them attributes: good, beautiful, divine. Values in this stage are projections of our feelings. The necessities of life are decisive factors behind our values. With the growth of this life, with the expansion of our mind, those necessities change, too, and transcend mere bodily demands. There is no biological need for the innumerable creations in science, art, music, religion, etc.. Behind those creations are our higher psychical and spiritual wants, which are not less vital than our physiological exigencies.

The genetic approach to values robs them of their absoluteness. Human creations are not finalities. To deplore this fact shows how deeply one has succumbed to metaphysics of values. Only to a believer in values as perfect essences, entities, could the discovery turn out to be a disappointment that they are merely human, all-too-human contingencies. As such they lose their fictitious, sublime properties, but driven from the "noumenal realm" they stop being "apparitions" and become realities. The fact that moral values are our creations proves that morality has its fundament in our own nature. Just as beauty is called into being because in our organization there is order and chaos, articulate and inarticulate stirrings, emotions, so goodness must have its roots in life itself. These roots lie in our gregarious potentialities. The assumption that man is an innately bellicose being, ("homo homini lupus") is a wrong, baseless and dangerous slogan, on which bloodthirsty tyrants, ruthless demagogues, insane criminals capitalized and still capitalize. Cases where one animal attacks and devours another of the same species are very rare. To say that such cases are a rule among men is preposterous. Most primitive tribes have their moral rules and norms which were not taken from the blue sky, but rather discovered as immanent forms of life itself.

Moral norms are either voluntarily executed or enforceable by various penalties. The first case indicates their appropriateness, the second their inappropriateness. The inappropriateness may disclose either an immoral derangement of our social impulses or their higher transformation. A criminal defies common rules because of his crippled social emotions; an apostle, a pioneer of humanity assails prevalent norms because his sociality has outgrown their narrowness. In science any advance is the result of a thorough assimilation of the old, and any new step is an addition to the perpetuating continuum of knowledge. Similarly in morality, any step forward is an increase of the accumulated wealth of values. Such a step leads to a richer, larger goodness. Like beauty and truth, goodness is variable in its incremental potentialities and possibilities. Its fundamental, invariable, essential characteristics are: respect for human life, consideration, temperance, sympathy and compassion for others, resentment against any malicious transgressor of human rights, etc.. Respecting and furthering the life of others means sustaining and enhancing our own life. Our self thrives and expands with the self of others, bodily and mentally.

For the reality of goodness and badness speaks our emotional response with pleasantness and unpleasantness which indicate that the former is beneficial, the latter detrimental. Our approval of good and disapproval of evil are not arbitrary responses, rather attitudes invoked by life itself. Behind our acclamation and admiration there is always gratification of our needs, elementary and higher. We respond with gratitude when our struggle for food and shelter is eased by our fellow men; our gratitude is heightened when our creative abilities can develop, attain fulfillment, by finding adequate outlets. Where goodness prevails, there, too, our interests, our aims, are enlarged, diverted from objectives of transient pleasure to ends whose realization offers inspiring happiness.

Behind our condemnation and abhorrence there is always pain, torture, inflicted on us or on other men. Our compassion, our sympathy with the sufferings of others do not come to life suddenly. They have their roots in our social impulses which have been cultivated in the course of years. Our responsiveness and kindness grow when we realize that sufferings of others may become ours at any time. Such comprehension does not degrade sympathy at all, but makes it a driving force against evil, near and distant, evil inflicted on our relatives, on our fellow men, on mankind. To be indifferent to murder, humiliation and misery, is callousness, selfishness. Selfishness is not only incarnate badness; it is also stupidity, ignorance.

Morally- relevant facts have led men to both moral values and disvalues. To bring these facts to clearer consciousness is the task of ethics as a science of moral life. Its result can never be a subjectivism of good and bad. Good and bad are not exclusive experiences of single individuals, they are common to all, at least in their fundamental meanings. There are different forms of goodness as there are various configurations of beauty; but their basic character remains the same. Coherence, consistency, integration, unity in variety, life-sustaining and life-furthering factors have been and are invariable qualities of values. Their change, effected by different economic and social circumstances, is not a modification of their formal characteristics. "Men's passions and wants may vary from age to age and according to the society in which they are to be satisfied. Accordingly, progress is possible in morality, though the formal character of morality does not change. There are, accordingly, no degrees of goodness at any one time nor as between different times. The widow's mite, to take the stock example, is as good and generous as the endowment of a hospital. A good Greek or Fijian is as good as a good Christian, though their approvals may and do vary. But though goodness does not differ in degree it may differ in largeness or greatness."[144] Our response to higher forms of goodness varies with our moral sense. Since we are not born in a social void, moral sense is more than an "hypothesis ad hoc," invented to explain moral conduct. It is a fact. No value could have been discovered if our impulses and passions were nothing but brute, chaotic forces. It is true that this discovery was the work of a few outstanding individuals; but what they revealed was something real. Revelations of a few may become common good if they are experimentally established.

The more we dwell in values, the better we become equipped to grasp them, to make them a part of our life. As in beauty, so in goodness, a mere emotional response is insufficient. Goodness appeals to our emotions and passions; but this appeal will be transient if we do not understand its social function in sustaining and incrementing life. The transition from emotions to moral judgments is a prerequisite of the experience of moral values.[145] Knowledge is the best means of cultivating our moral sense. Coming of age in morality is an act of reflective consciousness. The wider and deeper our knowledge, the more capable we are to clarify all those vague concepts of moral values which were implanted in our early childhood. Vague ideas are the source of social maladjustments. We cannot act right when we do not know what is right and what is wrong, what is good and what is bad. (In their moral sense, right and wrong, good and bad converge.)

Moral conduct is determined by motive "colored by a general attitude to life."[146] "An action is judged good or bad not by reference merely to its motive, but by a comparison of that with the whole range of motives that would ideally be present."[147] "It is the whole nature of that which I set to bring about, not that part of it which I happen to desire, that makes my act right or wrong."[148] "We must throw into the balance the weight of our whole self in what is called voluntary moral effort if we are to tip the scales of actions in favor of the higher but weaker alternative."[149] Whenever we judge a person as good or bad we must consider the whole character behind the particular act, which in turn cannot be isolated from the total context of experience. Intelligence and knowledge are our greatest assets in such estimations, and are decisive in our own moral conduct. No wonder that many thinkers who have tried to improve our morality by axioms, definitions have fallen in with the belief in a rationalistic, formalistic ethic. They had ignored the fact that principles, no matter how architectonically built, are futile and empty if not experimentally discovered.

Conscience, Sense Of Duty.

Moral values are not intrinsic values, "ends in themselves." We do not conform to goodness for goodness' sake, we conform to it as the most propitious form of life itself. In our mental and moral infantilism we needed taboos to harmonize our wants with those of others. In our coming of age in morality we realize that our self-fulfilment is intrinsically linked with the fulfilment of others. In extreme, asocial seclusion there is no self-preservation, still less self-expansion. Our impulses and passions when devoid of any noble aims (which are always social) turn either against ourselves or against others; and aggressiveness, murder, call for aggressiveness, murder on the part of others. A society of murderers is a "contradictio ad absurdum."

Social maladjustments have their main cause in an inadequate apprehension of moral values. If we are not guided by true patterns of life, our acts become blind responses to immediate situations; and whenever we do not plan, nor deliberate, and do not consider antecedents and consequences of our behavior, defeat is unavoidable. Without knowledge of the desirable objects, of the inspiring and frustrating aims, we fall from one passion into another, indulging in dubious, fleeting pleasures. Our happiness is as illusory as that of an insane man or drunkard, whose final lot is self-destruction.

To live in goodness is not only a virtue but also a

necessity. To be socially adjusted means to be well integrated, to procure for our self proper outlets for its dormant, creative potentialities. With our social emergence the fragmentary and rudimentary order in us develops, inchoate stirrings and emotions become articulate, passions are converted into purposive endeavors, from passive automata we grow into active centers. As with beauty and truth, so with goodness. Once we understand them as necessities of life, we cannot help but preserve and augment them. That values "should be appreciated," "produced," is an epiphenomenon of our value experience.[150] We speak of an "ought" (sollen) which devoid of its "metaphysical tinge" stands for comprehension of the functional significance of values. To say truth or goodness ought to be; means to be conscious of their practical relevance.[151]

Closely related to "ought" is our sense of duty. Duty is "sense socialized," "not sense restrained."[152] Duty which does not live in our emotions, passions, is an artifact of our intellect; and principles do not effect our morality unless our wants and impulses can attune and conform to them. The transition from opposition to a positive inclination of our passions to values is the fundament of morality. Due to it, our ability to form habits, norms, previously executed under pressure, become later on, immanent forms of our life. In this stage moral demands have the effect of appeals, obligations turn into dispositions. We prefer acts of duty performed without an inner struggle of competing motives, to acts of duty executed with struggle if they concern the most necessary requirements of morality. Higher forms of moral life cannot be actualized without a constant struggle and conflict of motives. Morally excellent deeds call for immense sacrifices. It is, after all, not the ease in performance, but the nature of the aim or ideal, that attests moral greatness.

Our impulses, passions, habits, no matter how refined they may be, are insufficient implements to cope with ever changing conditions and situations. We need reason in our adjustments and readjustments. Reason cultivates our sense of duty, our conscience, and effects its transition from irrational fluctuations to rational determination. The voice of such a penetrating and discerning conscience is indispensable in all those situations which call for an enlarging of our values. It is here that morality begins to be creative. "Creative morality is embodiment in intentional action of deeply and widely significant good."[153] Its individual form does not make of goodness a subjective value, provided it conforms to the general characteristics of goodness. Any artistic work differs from any other by virtue of its unique expression; and yet there are features common to all which render them beautiful. With moral acts it is the same.

Moral values direct and redirect us in the conforming and harmonizing of our wants and aims with those of others. In order to conform we must guide our passions, divert them from immediate, dubious ends to distant, larger and nobler objectives. Our impulses and passions are genuine in their vitality but not in their acquired ways of acting. To say that good life is weak, less vital, is nothing short of nonsense. As beauty does not decrease the dynamic of our psychic life but rather increases it, so it is with goodness. Converted passions are not limited in their growth, expansion; whereas unrestricted blind passions, by being tied down to immediate objects flare up quickly, but die quickly too. Cases from current clinical psychology reveal weakness of will, inferior mentality, cowardice as dominant factors behind crime.

Moral values depict all those "intakings" and "outgivings" of which social life consits. They are our privileges and our obligations. When we realize that our own self expands by its social emergence, that the "obligation, which we look upon as a bond between men, first binds us to ourselves,"[154] that coherence, consistency, integration, order, are our necessities, we cannot help but shield and promote those patterns of life which implement them. A selfish, ruthless, asocial life has no advantages when man wakes up to his fundamental rights to live, to thrive and expand. It is the impotence and stupidity of those who endure injustice, intolerance and murder which encourage scoundrels, rascals in their devilish doing.

Any change is bad when it leads to disorder, chaos, "every code of rules is better than none;"[155] but when we visualize a better order, we must strive for it. Tradition is necessary; but when tradition is built on errors, wrong beliefs, prejudices, it is our moral duty to discard all of its retarding elements. Science cannot advance without the accumulated wealth of knowledge. Neither can science develop if we sanction given achievements as ultimate attainments. In art, morality and religion it is the same.

APPENDIX A

On "Fate"

The ancient Greeks and Romans thought of fate as a transcendent power which determines all events. Celestial movements, birth and death, good and bad endowments, poverty and prosperity, vicissitudes in human lot, were thought of as decreed by "Fate," conceived of as divine personifications (Moirae or Parcae). Apart from such mythological explanations, "Fate" or "Necessity" was thought of as identical with the "chaotic matter" as something entirely opposite to mind. All evils: sickness, cataclysms of nature, earthquakes, bodily and physical tribulations, and all kinds of dread experiences were ascribed to this brute, raw matter as the inevitable lot of created nature.

Since human life was imagined to be intimately bound up with celestial movements, astrology became the most celebrated pseudo-science among all ancient peoples, and, unfortunately, still enjoys its old reputation. The variety of characters was linked with star-emanations or fluids and all kinds of astrological symbols were invented to account for it. Men fell in with the belief in this pseudo-science which promised to reveal their future, and, what is more, their future in rosy colors, such as good fortune. Anyone who knew how to satisfy this infantile desire, by interpreting "visions" in the clouds and "unusual" voices in the night, became a celebrity.

"Fate," as "Necessity," or "all-pervading logos" (Stoa) inspired man in his endeavor to find natural laws. Apart from that, the influence of the idea of the transcendent fate was a devastating one. If our life, and the forms it takes in the course of years, is the outcome of some metaphysical entity, according to which everything that happens is bound to happen, and no change can be effected by human efforts, then what wonder that a fatalistic indifference became the common reaction.

One of the noblest accomplishments of the Renaissance was the idea of the immanent fate. Man lost his interest in metaphysical speculations and began to concentrate his energies on finding the causal nexus of events. Natural science has developed since then at a pace never dreamed of before. The empirical point of view has become predominant and a thorough study of facts has led directly to the discovery of the fundamental laws of nature. Inquiries into human behavior have helped man to realize that social evils are not beyond remedy.

The concept of the immanent fate has been a tremendous creative asset. If man's destiny is formed and reformed by man, it is for us to make this destiny one of greatness and dignity. Tyranny, misery, intolerance, injustice, race and caste barriers, wherever they thrive, are a Cain's mark on society, a crime which humanity commits against itself. We are living in times where too much stress is being put on economic forces and circumstances, and very little on the power of ideas. Primitive beliefs and tendencies have often made the history of mankind a bloody record of battles, battles of blind passion against blind passion, battles void of any noble ends. Ignorance and superstition have been the enemy of man. Wherever progress is retarded, they are at work; wherever human suffering is immense, they are behind it; wherever hatred is fanned to murder, they are the acting evil. If we obscure the mind of the people by ideas taken from a barbaric period, what wonder when one day the same people turn out to be barbarians again? Whoever talks about fate as though it were the unchangeable decree of a metaphysical power prolongs man's misery and enforces his retrogression.

The fact that the same event becomes "fateful" for one individual, and may affect another very little, if at all, dismisses the old idea of fate as something external, entirely independent of us. If events affect different characters in various ways, we must look to character itself as one of the fate-determining factors. Sickness, death of beloved ones, failures, hardships, disappointments in love and friendship, have never been experienced in the same way by all. What turns out to be a tragic conflict for one individual passes without enduring impression on another. A single dread experience in our daily life may incapacitate us for the rest of our lives, or we may emerge with renewed strength. Many a man or woman never stops lamenting about growing old, while the majority take it as matter of course. Infidelity may make us misanthropes, or may be taken as one of the many fortuitous incidents.

Our physical and mental constitution is the driving

force in determining which situations and circumstances of the outer world shall become decisive. Fateful events are not fateful in themselves. They become fateful through a particular character. Our passions and interests play an important role in all those events which turn out to be fateful. What appears as strange coincidence, or as an act of "mysterious" fate, loses all of its ominous meaning as soon as we become conscious of our propensities and habits. There is good reason to believe that with the progress of psychology and sociology the "inexplicable" in human behavior will be traced down to elements apt to a rational analysis. Today we are well informed about phenomena which not long ago were unknown. That our dreams reveal our moral and mental state has been a great discovery. Of no less importance is the comprehension of such character-building elements as undercurrents of society, atavistic influences and unconscious contents.

What form our life has been taking in the course of years, the quality and intensity of our conflicts, depend to a high degree, upon what particular character we have arrived at. When we study the history of great men and reflect upon their "fate," we know that environment, hardships, poverty and social barriers are limitations we cannot gloss over. They have been great obstacles that impede our development and force upon us unnecessary struggles. The nature of their impact depends upon the character that battles them. Many men come out of this battle victorious. Will-power and persisting interests have been the driving forces in the realization of the ideals they were inspired by. Those men were not favored by any mysterious fate, or destiny, and did not consult horoscopes to find out what the future had in store for them.

There is reciprocal causation between environment and our character. Just as life forms our character, so character makes this life a unique one. Character is not something fixed which we receive as a heritage. It is molded by education, environment, social beliefs and patterns. Once our character becomes rigid, our behavior, our habits, our interests, aims and ways of realization established, the course of our experiences will show a similar trend. Our intimate circle will be composed of the same kind of people, no matter where we live; our social affairs will be disposed of in the same manner, similar surprises and disappointments will not be rare. We are inclined to project this fixed line of life and hypostatize it to "fate" or "destiny."

Our attitude towards the problem of fate reveals our personality. Whether we conceive of fate as something independent of us (in whatsoever form as the impact of the outer world or some metaphysical power, or as the outcome of the reciprocal determination of objective and subjective constituents of our life), will depend on whether we are of a predominantly passive or active type. The passive type projects his own inactivity and uses the iron law of fate as an escape and excuse for his own shortcomings. He blames everything but himself for defeat. He may indulge in the gratification of primitive needs; or grasping its transitory worth, become the blackest pessimist and despair of humanity. The active type believes in the immanence of fate, which belief is deeply rooted in his unfolding, constructive urges. He is always conscious of the important part character plays in shaping our life, and is averse to ascribe success or failure to blind chance or ominous, impersonal factors. The highest among the active is the creative type, if he is imbued and driven by ideals of great ethos. He never questions human values because he bears them in himself, and a better society is for him an inward certainty, given as vision, and an indomitable will for calling it into being. The passion for an ideal can become so powerful that it may kill all other interests. This obsession is often experienced as an external force. Many a great man talks of himself as an instrument of a higher might — "fate" — which is, in reality, nothing but a projected inner constellation.

CHAPTER VI

RELIGIOUS VALUES

"The essentially unreligious attitude is that which attributes human achievement to man in isolation from the world of physical nature and his fellows."[156]

Man aspires to a total world-outlook. Out of this vital, transcending urge religion sprang to life and evolves in close connection with the entire experience. Religious values are real in the psychic dynamic which they sustain and augment, in the coherence and consistency of our emotions and thoughts, in the social bonds, in the intellectual and moral communion they nurture and propagate. They are not "intrinsic" entities of a "noumenal" realm. Religion which subscribes to such supernatural "essences" does not move along with life, and becomes obsolete and dogmatic, and achieves the opposite of what it intends. A constant revision of values is necessary to avoid their petrification. Science does it, theology does it, too, in its attempt to espouse faith with an objectivity indicative of the unbiased spirit of scientific research. "What else is the meaning of the great labors of historical criticism as applied to its sacred scriptures by religious leaders themselves, of the acceptance of scientific accounts of the creation of the world and of men, with the candid dismissal of old myths and superstitions?"[157]

130

The biggest mistake atheism makes is the confusion of facts with interpretations of facts. Religious values are "values of actual experience,"[158] not artificial products which we can add to or subtract from life arbitrarily. Our life expands, and with this process goes a transformation of values, a transition from simple to more complex forms. We do not become anti-scientists because truth itself has undergone such a change. Why do it in religion? Suppose we find that concepts of God, soul, immortality, which were regarded as valid by our ancestors turn out to be vague ideas, incongruent with reality. Can we, on account of this discovery, deny the real facts which lie behind these concepts? An atheistic approach shares with any dogmatic theology its ontological aspect. It decrees: because there is no proof of the existence of God as a personal, transcendent being, we must discard the idea of God altogether. But behind the concept of God is our enhanced spiritual activity. Religiously-relevant facts lead us to religious values. No matter how "enlightened" we become, how superior we deem ourselves as compared to our remote ancestors in their trials and gropings, we face similar problems. The loss of beloved ones does not invoke transient feelings, or sneering, cynical attitudes. We are overwhelmed by grief and sadness and begin to meditate. We cannot help but look for something to hold on to in our distress. Death is an eternal problem with which we must cope. We may deride old beliefs in a soul and its immortality; but we cannot extirpate our urge to survive. Our knowledge is fragmentary. Whatsoever solution we may find, new and more difficult problems follow. And yet we aspire to total knowledge. Out of this surging impulse we progress; things unknown to-day may become known tomorrow. Were we content with given achievements, we could never boast of any achievement.

True science does not discard faith, but makes for its better foundation. The more we know, the more reasons we find for feeling our insignificance and littleness in the vast universe. The geocentric world-outlook was awe-inspiring. Still more so is the discovery that our earth is only a tiny body among millions of others. Our sense of humility and dependence was not weakened; rather, it was strengthened by the revelation of the immense energies of nature. We have conquered fear of an unknown universe, but "fear never gave stable perspectives in the life of anyone."[159] With our unflagging faith in the power of reason, with our untiring inquiries into things and events, with graspings of our shortcomings and efficiencies, we no longer indulge in "theodicees" or "kosmodicees." Atheistic nihilistic, unreligious attitudes spring from such naive interpretations. It is difficult to find a way out of confusions and pseudo-questions which erroneous interpretations of religious facts impose. To declare God an omnipotent, omniscient, transcendent being, who engenders and guides our actions, means, indeed, proclaiming him responsible for the evils committed by ourselves. No less devoid of facts is the division of reality into two worlds, the world of phenomena and the world of noumena, the realm of causal determination and the realm of absolute indetermination (Kant). If we try to divide what is not divisible, if we separate reality and value, no wonder that the quotient does not work. With values as supertemporal essences we are at a loss. They simply do not fit into our life; and besides, we conform to norms and patterns that spring from life itself rather than to external entities. By realizing that values are our own creations, we are encouraged to transform them into more appropriate, more propitious increments. Which forms are adequate is not given to everyone to discover, any more than it is given to reveal the laws of nature. Religious geniuses, prophets, penetrate deeply into nature and human behavior and reveal through their creations what is common to man.[160] Findings of a few become communicable and shareable if they are experimentally established. The fact that their revelations must often wait centuries to be accepted is due to human inertia and ignorance. There is no better proof of the reality of their discoveries than their survival despite slaughter and persecution incited by impostors and charlatans. We may regard skeptically the current gospels about these living paragons of humanity, but cannot question their own teachings and actions. They were great men through their deeds and sacrifices. They ignored obstructions, risked their lives, to raise the dignity of man by serving God.

We like to talk about our beliefs as intimate, private affairs. But a faith that does not manifest itself in behavior is no faith at all. It is blasphemy, tartuffery. By our deeds we can demonstrate whether we believe in God or not. Were religion experienced and comprehended in its true and vital dynamic, many human tragedies could have been avoided. We are all wicked at the core if we make a distinction between faith and actions, a division which leads to toleration and perpetuation of evil. We cannot serve God while we trample human rights under our feet. Such service is lip service, irreligion in its worst form.

Religious values grow with other values. As little as we can substitute economic values for religious, so little can we replace religious values by economic ones. A "coalescence"[161] of values is the precondition of a salutary social life. No economic improvements will eradicate murder, injustice, intolerance, if man remains wicked. To be wicked means to be without faith, be it faith in God as the transcending, perpetuating human spirit, or faith in the dignity of man, in ideals. Not out of hybris, contentment, did science grow, but out of felt and apprehended shortcomings, insufficiencies; and religious values point to these with the same vigor as other values do. Not the sodden and bloated impostors, wicked tyrants, who thought of themselves as omnipotent masters liberated man from darkness, but the creative, modest geniuses who suffered with the human lot and saw behind man's "omnipotence" a misguided impotence. Humility before God should not be confused with humility before man. Piety, reverence, worship attached to frail and abject ends become irreligious expressions. It is the nature of the objective which renders our emotions religious or unreligious.

Mysticism.

"There is a state of mind, known to religious men, but to no others, in which the will to ourselves and hold our own has been displaced by a willingness to close our mouths and be as nothing in the floods and waterspouts of God. In this state of mind, what we most dreaded has become the habitation of our safety, and the hour of our moral death has turned into spiritual birthday. The time for tension in our soul is over, and that of happy relaxation, of calm deep breathing, of an eternal present, with no discordant future to be anxious about, has arrived. Fear is not held in abeyance as it is by mere morality, it is positively expunged and washed away."[162]

Mysticism finds its sole justification as a vital trend against extreme rationalism by pointing to the emotional source of religion. But emotions alone have never led to true discoveries, not in science, not in art, nor in religion. Even Bergson, who espouses mysticism so ardently and says, "mysticism and religion" are like "cause and effect," admits that mystic love "is neither of the senses nor of the mind, it is of both."[163] To assume that there are two kinds of emotions — "below and above" — the intellect,[164] is erroneous. Emotions are weak or intense, transient or enduring. Their noble or ignoble character is a property of the ends to which they are attached and the choice of these objectives is determined by reason.

Mysticism opens the road to skepticism and atheism. To claim "eternal" truths which can only be grasped by some higher sense, the exclusive gift of a few, is to render such truths very dubious phenomena. Real discoveries need more than emotional "drunkenness;" they exact untiring inquiries into the nature of events, shifting of attention from trivial to momentous occurrences, resourceful planning and looking ahead. In all those activities we are guided by reason. It is important to be conscious of our vital impulses, passions and emotions. An overestimation of them is dangerous. Irrationalism leads to retrogression.

Romanticism was a sound reaction against dogmatic and rigid classicism, but became a failure in its extreme character. Realism and naturalism followed in due course. We cannot make irrationalism into a permanent perspective of life. Without reason we indulge in illusions, and mistake these frail deceptions of our wants for realities. We need reason which keeps abreast of new discoveries and appraises given patterns of life as to their beneficial results. Emotions and impulses may outgrow established, conventional forms, but can never open our eyes to better, more propitious adjustments. Science does not progress through irrational methods. We know well into what discredit philosophy fell on account of the romanticism of Hegel and Schelling in their adventurous approach to natural events. Speculations devoid of facts are useless encumbrances.

With religion it is not different. To discard reason because in our dogmatic rigidity we may adhere to obsolete values is to confuse effects with causes. Behind our firm holding on there is no reasoning, but beliefs and tendencies, deeply rooted in our passions and habits. As a rule, the less founded our beliefs, the more obstinate and recalcitrant we are in defending them. "It is easier to wean a miser from his hoard, than a man from his deeper opinions,"[165] especially, when these beliefs are rooted in prejudices, or wishful thinking. To employ reason does not mean inventing justifications for our doing; rather, testing it empirically, looking ahead to its consequences and examining the whole context of the particular act.

To embody intelligence in actions is "to convert casual, natural goods, whose causes and effects are unknown, into goods valid for thought, right for conduct and cultivated for appreciation."[166] Reason is a critical method which directs us "to more secure goods, turning assent and assertion into free communication of shareable meanings, turning feeling into ordered and liberal sense, turning reaction into response."[167]

The Objectivity Of Religious Values.

Religious values do not denote "ends in themselves," spiritual noumena, independent of us, but immanent forms of life. Their validity is a matter of experience. The way they operate, their role in sustaining and enhancing life, is decisive. In this respect they are not distinguished from other values. The fact that our own creations have beneficial results in our adaptation to nature and social adjustments speaks for their reality. If we forget the functional significance of values and mistake them for ontological, fixed realities, they turn into lifeless rigid principles, and, as such, appear entirely inadequate to cope with all those fluid situations which changing economic and social conditions bring forth. Because values are real they evolve. That the goodness, beauty and holiness of certain generations turn out too narrow and primitive for other generations does not confirm values as adventitious interpretations of irrelevant facts. Similar facts call for like explanations. But facts are not stable. Primitive and more civilized people face different facts. And among the same people there are individuals of a wide and rich orbit and others of a narrow and poor horizon. It is only a matter of course that their moral and religious experiences should be different. Various experiences call for diverse representations. Therefore, religion has always employed manifold techniques for communicating religious values. Music, architecture, processions, rites, prayers, and sacraments, have been such effective stimuli.

Religious values are social patterns. In complete isolation there is no beauty, goodness or holiness. Man in the course of his social expansion found better means of sustaining life and of enlarging it by giving physical embodiments to his experiences. Through these objectified forms tradition perpetuates itself. There is no advance without tradition, without the accumulated wealth of values. "Ours is the responsibility of conserving, transmitting and expanding the heritage of values we have received that those who come after us may receive it more solid and secure, more widely accessible and more generously shared than we have received."[168] Illiteracy in religion is as bad as illiteracy in general. Any step forward is conditioned by a thorough assimilation of given achievements. To discover, to comprehend and to live up to better forms we must know those which have become inadequate. If there are vital needs which have led man to religion, it is important to get acquainted with all objectified expressions which have gratified his wants. By not knowing them we may revive beliefs of our remote ancestors and repeat their trials and failures over and over.

History of religion has its forward and backward trends. We find highest ideals and mean idols, enthusiasm for sublime purposes and blind fanaticism attached to abject ends; spiritual pervasion and "the spirit of corporate dominion;"[169] true service of God coupled with service of Satan, proper religion and pseudo-religion. To separate them is a vital necessity. Can we blame science for the misdeeds of impostors who propagate fallacies vestured in scientific terms, in order to disguise their ruthless, destructive aims? Can we blame religion for persecutions, inquisitions, tortures, hatred, aggressiveness carried on in the name of God by charlatans, wicked demagogues? Let us not commingle those vile beasts with great religious men who became saints as creators of values, as "impregnators of the world, vivifiers and animators of potentialities of goodness, which but for them would lie forever dormant."[170] Out of this confusion came the sharp distinction between religion as personal attitude and religion as sum of beliefs, publicly espoused. This division neglects the social aspects of religious institutions. The latter provide us with many "opportunities for participating in the life of a public group," and thus convey "a sense of social dignity."[171] Religious institutions, being conscious of their social role, must take care that religion unite rather than divide us. Their teaching and living up to the true religious spirit make for their sacredness. We find in public places of worship elated stimuli for pious experiences which are not exclusively confined to them. After all "most celebrated epiphanies are reported to have occurred not in temples and services, but in stables and fields. . ."[172]

We call religious values supreme or total to accentuate their significance in our attitudes toward the world and our fellow men. Piety that does not color our actions is a very transient feeling. No less evanescent is holiness which we apprehend only in religious institutions. We are acting beings, and values express our attitudes, the degree of our coherence, consistency, integration. By separating religious values from other values we render religion the worst service. Religion falls into discredit when it tries to keep itself aloof, when instead of being a vital pervasion of our singular acts, it sees its task in an exclusive service of supernatural forces. Faith that chooses another subject than life itself becomes an encumbrance. Faith that consoles us with celestial rewards, and teaches submission to evil instead of resisting and eradicating it, has a short-lived appeal.

True religion is creative as true morality is. Bergson speaks of two societies, a closed and an open one, of two religions, a static and dynamic; Montague speaks of belief "unbound." They mean the same. Behind rigid forms there is always a disguised disorder. Life changes, and this transition calls for a a steady revision of values. Faith which is more than blind imitation of transmitted beliefs and tendencies will be unbound, able to develop, to rejuvenate. We would still have paganism if not for the social awakening of those few religious geniuses who took up the struggle against the evil in man, against inertia which yielded "under their impulsion."[173] In their devotion to God they raised human dignity by calling into being potentialities of a richer life. The universality of faith they taught and lived was a spiritual universality. From them we may learn that "man manifests universality in religion, not by possessing the one faith in which all may be led to entire good, but by the character of certain spheres of his interests and activity."[174] Faith that makes man "whole" must permeate our acting and thinking. Such a faith is never attached to a particular, tribal or national holiness which feeds intolerance, fanaticism, pugnacity, ignorance and superstition.

Holiness.

Like all other spiritual values, religious values denote "actual growth of one's very being," they are "increments of psychic substance"[175] and differ from each other "not merely in intensity but in volume and depth."[176] Piety, reverence, grace, blessedness, holiness are not passive states of mind in which we grasp some eternal, cosmic entity, but activities in which values are created or re-created when they are given in objectified forms. Such enhanced activities make for a richer life. In our spiritual expanding, religious values are not less important than aesthetic and moral values. They give coherence to our fragmentary, inarticulate stirrings and emotions, and operate as ends in view in the actualization of our potentialities. To the social ties of beauty and goodness holiness adds new ones. Love, that knows no limits in growth, finds its highest affirmation in religion which opens our eyes to noble ends and ideals, and keeps our interests alive. Our faith in the indomitable human spirit finds in religious experience a source of vital energies. Faith in humanity is intimately bound up with faith in nature that "is making for values."[177] Science does not discourage such a belief. It only curbs our "cosmic gropings." We do not indulge in speculations any more about nature as the incarnation of a "divine power" or "world spirit." Such metaphysical fancies are doomed to failure. Sickness, death, cataclysms of nature, evils, etc., remain living reminders not to face facts with illusions. But man has gradually learned to improve his lot, and there is good reason for hoping that he will progress in this direction, and will harness vast natural energies for better use. Religion sustains such hopes by pointing to our cosmic interdependence.

What is the nature of the psychic dynamic of "holiness"? Rudolf Otto[178] elaborates on this concept and his findings help us realize that emotional and cognitive elements are fused together in our higher religious experiences. He makes a distinction between the "numinous" and the "holy." The former is devoid of any rational components, the latter has cognitive constituents. With the "holy" we describe our emotions attached to an objective of supreme moral and mental qualities, be it God, the Divine or Deity. The "numinous" is the pristine "holy," lacking its rational determinants. It is an intense emotional response, whose object is a hypostatization of feelings in the form of such ideas as: tremendum, majestas, energicum, fascinans, mirum and sanctum. Such vehement feelings without distinct cognitive objectives are very common among the mentally deranged. We call them residua of our archaic state of mind.[179] Emotions without distinct cognitive elements flare up and die quickly.

Intensity of feeling does not indicate a value if there is no harmonious integration of other psychic functions. Whoever narrows down religious values to emotional responses weakens "the forces of religious progress" and opens the "door to irrational extravagancies."[180] What makes an emotion into a religious expression is the nature of the object to which it is attached, and the noble or the ignoble character of such an end cannot be determined save by reason. Faith by which we live and grow is faith cultivated by critical intelligence. Credo quia absurdum this beloved mystical motto is not the right path to religion. Inconsistency in thoughts leads to inconsistency in actions. We cannot trust reason in one field and distrust it in another. A God in whom we cannot believe with reason is a frail idol, and faith based exclusively on emotions is as transient as a cloud.

God.

The deeper reason for employing the same concepts, although their functional significance varies, lies in the continuity of our spiritual life. Our present is not a discrete temporal fraction. It is a part of the past and emerges constantly into the future. With any step forward we must incorporate, assimilate, previous experiences which in turn determine new ones. Our personal history is an insignificant fragment of the perpetually evolving human tradition. This continuity explains our persistent abiding by certain ideas. Ideas which endure are fundamental concepts. Science applies them, art does it, morality and religion too. Matter, energy, time, space, causality, are typical of the ideas natural science will never dispense with. Beauty, proportion, unity in variety, are few of the most important aesthetic notions. Good, bad, noble, mean, are valuations no morality can drop. Grace, holiness, God, are pivotal concepts of every religion.

The historical modifications of our religious values prove beyond doubt that they are not factitious attachments to life, but are organically fused with the transformation of these needs. The genealogy of religion shows that religious values are neither initial nor final, that they are derived from experience and evolve with experience. The attempt to elucidate present values exclusively on the basis of their "primordial" expressions is doomed to failure. Brightman speaks of the "fallacy of primitivism."[181] The most pristine religious life is rather complex, and we cannot conjure our remote ancestors to answer questions related to our time. It is the "fallacy of primitivism" that has led many thinkers to generalizations, such as: "fear created God," or "religion has its origin in the feeling of dependence," etc.. Even pristine religious experiences are intricate. Behind them are many impulses, various patterns of socializing, and diverse aspirations to a total world-outlook.

Atheism overlooks the complex character of religious life, and ignores the transition of our vital needs which are behind it. To deny God because our ancestors had vague religious ideas, relative to their time and to their mental level, is as little justified as skepticism in science on account of its past gropings. We today, with our advanced knowledge, face problems similar to those of our ancestors. Suffering, sickness, death, natural and social evils, have not lost one of their piercing and tormenting pains. Our orbit has become richer and wider, and because of this our fundamental religious ideas have changed to forms more appropriate to encompass the modified psychic dynamic for which they stand. Our God has stopped being a particular, tribal idol, or a personified transcendent entity, hovering above us with no concern for human misery. God has become a "repository of human values . . . embodiment of goodness and righteousness,"[182] a symbol of the unity "of all ideal ends arousing us to desire and actions,"[183] an "active relation between ideal and actual."[184] Whatsoever great creative men we reflect upon, we find behind their doing a strong conviction that their finite role is somehow compensated for by the perpetuation of the human mind. God as the infinite spirit is the expression of the strength we derive from our social emergence. In isolation we are frail; as moral and social units we are strong, and touch God in our noble endeavors and heroic struggles for a better and more dignified humanity.

APPENDIX B

On "Race"

When we reflect upon the facts to which the concept of race can be traced, we are appalled by the ruthless theories the racists have been able to propagate. Indeed, not a single one of their vicious and harmful beliefs can be verified, and it will remain a disgrace to humanity that these charlatans have found and still find millions of followers. The reasons for this are many and of a very intricate nature. Sciences which deal with human beings, their psychic and mental structure and behavior, trail far behind the natural sciences. To this fact we usually get a ready-made answer. Natural sciences deal with repetitious events; human actions happen but once, they are unpredictable. This statement cannot be taken at its face value. Repetition and causal determination are not exclusive properties of natural events. They apply to us too. We could hardly live in a social world of causal indetermination. We could neither plan nor perform an action, neither adjust nor readjust ourselves. It is true, our predictions concerning human behavior have not such a high degree of probability as those related to natural events. But the fault is largely with ourselves. While we hold on to the fundamental requirement of experimental testing in natural sciences we are too credulous in sociology, ethnology, anthropology, and mistake speculations for facts. After all, behind such conjectures and guessings are our own beliefs and tendencies, our prejudiced opinions presented in the form of scientific terms. Such concocted rubbish is the fanciful edifice of the racists who take advantage of the paucity of data related to the origin and variety of the races, and invent pseudo-facts, the refutation of which is impossible by all who are not thoroughly acquainted with true scientific findings. It is no wonder that such speculations grow without end. After all, they depend upon the personality of their creator, on his temperament, mentality, and other factors, such as social position. A bellicose man will talk about innate pugnacity and espouse it as a high virtue; a moral decadent will glorify ruthlessness, selfishness. Ignorant individuals, frustrated in one way or another, will give their passions an outlet by inciting hatred of others, will teach the subtleness of sheer power, aggressiveness, fury, revenge and discrimination, and will invent the myth of the superiority of their own race. Slave traders, in order to find a justification for their devilish doings, will propagate theories on the genuine and unchangeable inferiority of the exploited slaves.

It is always a sound principle to study the man who intends to inculcate us with his obscure beliefs. Let us, for example, have a closer look at Gobineau, the founder of racism. The very fact that he dedicates his two volumes about the "Inequality of Human Races" to the blind German king George V. of Hanover must make us suspicious. George V. destroyed relentlessly the liberal constitution his father granted. Can we imagine a man of intellectual integrity and fairness towards his fellow men shaking hands with a tyrant, a reactionary despot who trampled fundamental human rights under his feet? Can we assume that a man who knows well that social classes have evolved in the course of centuries, himself believes in the nonsense of an aristocracy by birth? Such a man is not interested in truth, but in preserving his own privileges by disseminating fallacies, furbished with pseudo-scientific ideas. No more awe-inspiring are Houston Chamberlain, Madison Grant and the countless Hitlerites who debased science and converted its servants to wilful caterers to human misery. Their teachings are not based on facts.

The concept of race is a vague idea and a very harmful one, as the wholesale slaughter committed by Hitler and his stooges demonstrated. What are the real and what the imaginary facts related to race? "From the standpoint of a classificatory view of mankind which has due regard for the facts it is possible to recognize four distinctive stocks or divisions of mankind. These are the Negroid or black, the Archaic white or Australoid, the Caucasoid or white, and the Mongoloid stocks or divisions of mankind. It is preferable to speak of the varieties of men which enter into the formation of these divisions as ethnic groups. The use of this term of division emphasizes the fact that we are dealing with a major group of mankind sufficiently distinguishable in its physical characters from the three other major groups of mankind to be classified separately."[185] These different traits: color of the skin, form and bodily distribution of the hair, body build, etc., are the results of an extended, successful adaptation to the environment, and do not account for cultural varieties.

The pseudo-scientific theories of the racists are flagrant fallacies. There are only a few traits which entitle us to speak of races as subdivisions of human species. Those separating traits are very small as compared to our common characteristics which prove the essential unity of mankind. All groups have the same cultural potentialities, the realization of which depends upon environmental circumstances, favorable economic and social factors, salutary tradition and sound education. Due to these elements mental achievements vary among nations and within the same nation. "Heredity takes no notice of the glories of civilization, whether they are in science or in technology or in art, these can be perpetuated in any group, not by nature, but by nurture."[186] The highest level has never been reached by a group as a whole, but by a few outstanding individuals. Such prominent people we find among all nations. The most superficial perusal of our history shows that all ethnic groups have contributed to civilization. In fact, the basic advances were made by the people of the Orient when Europe was still very backward.[187]

We mention the racist invention of the Aryan "race" with reluctance, because it is the sheerest nonsense, and speaks against those millions of followers, of yesterday and today, who accepted it and continue to accept it as an established fact. The Aryan race exists only in the brains of ignorants. It has no factual reference to any particular Nordic race. Aryan is a linguistic term, a name for a group of languages such as: Sanscrit of ancient India, German, English, Slavic, Greek, Lithuanian, Albanian, etc..

To prove their humbug about superior and inferior races, the racists indulge in all kinds of human measurements. The commonest among them has been the cephalic index. From verifiable data we can see that the size and form of the brain do not differ among races and nations. The same group shows the narrowest and the broadest skulls; and concerning the size of the brain the differences are not smaller. When we bear in mind that the paleolithic Neanderthal man had a capacity of the skull of 1625 cc., that is, 175 cc. more than the average modern white man, we need not ponder the relationship between brain size and cultural achievements.[188] It simply does not exist. The biological fundaments for mental processes are alike among all human groups. No proof has ever been made of race differences in mentality.[189] "Mental capacity cannot be measured in avoirdupois ounces on the scale. The brain does not secrete cultural or intellectual power in the same way that the liver secretes bile. One is not born with the ability to think brilliantly. Such an ability can be brought about only by exposure of the brain and nervous system to, and education in, the proper conditions."[190]

Do we find any valid biochemical differences among human divisions? There are none, and any assumed consanguinity is fictitious. The "myth of blood goes back to time before Mendel, when heredity was thought in terms of inheritance of blood, when people believed that parental blood gives rise to the blood of the child."[191] The blood of all human beings is the same, that is, it has the same biochemical structure, and from a purely scientific point of view blood can have no other meaning. Our blood differs only in its agglutinating qualities, by virtue of which we distinguish four blood groups. None of these is the exclusive property of a single nation.

The racist reveals an almost incredible ignorance of matters concerning heredity. His greatest fallacy is the belief that we inherit fixed characters and not, as modern science has proved beyond any doubt, its constituent elements. These units are the genes, which form in larger aggregation the microscopically visible chromosomes. The genes determine the growth, weight and specific characteristics such as pigmentation and bodily potentialities, and condition our brain structure and gland functions. They are in a steady process of internal rearrangement. Due to the internal rearrangements of genes heredity cannot be thought of as absolute. Its course shows variations, sudden departures from type (mutations).

We inherit only the rough structure of our character, its dormant possibilities and potentialities which are constantly shaped by external circumstances. Optimal environmental conditions bring to full realization good potentialities which are preponderant. The percentage of hereditary mental defectives in every population is very small. To prove the innate inferiority of a national group, we must show that it was and is given the same economic, social and educational opportunities as the assumed higher group enjoys. Such a proof has never and never will be made, for the simple reason, that biologically and mentally, inherited potentialities are alike among all human divisions. The existing cultural, moral and mental differences are results of various experiences, diverse environmental influences. "When we get about the fact that such differences, whether small or great, depend mainly on external circumstances, it will be difficult to work up real hatred against other people."[192] True science, contrary to the corrupted, vitiated pseudo-science of the racists, reveals that the dissimilarities between nations are insignificant as compared with their similarities. In our fundamental traits, in our vital needs, in our sadness and gladness, in our tribulations and consolations, in the vicissitudes of our lot we are all alike.

The backward trends which we face today are very discouraging, but need not lead to despair if we realize that no epoch has been free of them. Thoughts of a uniformly golden age lack any foundation. An epoch becomes uniform only in retrospect. Scoundrels, impostors, have always been busy spreading evil, and have not hesitated to incite to murder to satisfy their ignoble aims. The best defense against evils inflicted on humanity by men themselves is eternal vigilance against any forced retrogression into a primitive mode of thinking. Discrimination against social groups, creed, nationalistic conceit, have been and are fed on ignorance, on the revival of old ideas, highly incongruent with reality.

BIBLIOGRAPHY

Abel Walter, Representation and Form, New York, 1936.
Alexander Samuel, Moral Order and Progress, Trubner & Co., London, 1889.
Art and Instinct, Clarendon Press, Oxford, 1921.
Beauty and other Forms of Value, Macmillan & Co. London, 1933.
(Value (in Bulletin of the John Ryland Library, vol. 17).
Ashley-Montagu Montague, F., Man's Most Dangerous Myth: The Fallacy of Race, Columbia Univ. Press, New York, 1945.
Benedict Ruth, Race: Science and Politics, The Viking Press, New York, 1945.
Bergson Henri, The two Sources of Morality and Religion, H. Henry Holt & Co., London, 1935.
Bleuler Eugen, Naturgeschichte der Seele und ihres Bewusstwerdens, Berlin, 1921.
Boas Franz, The Mind of the Primitive Man, Macmillan & Co., New York, 1938.
Race and Democratic Society, Augustin, New York, 1945.
Boodin John E., Philosophy of History (in Twentieth Century Philosophy), Philosophical Library, New York, 1943.
Brightman Edgar Sh., A Philosophy of Religion, Prentice Hall Inc., New York, 1940.
Carnap Rudolf, Philosophy and Logical Syntax, Paul, Trench, Trubner & Co., London, 1935.
Dahlberg Gunnar, Race, Reason and Rubbish, Allen & Unwin, London, 1942.
Dewey John, Experience and Nature, Open Court Publ. Co., Chicago, 1926.
Ethics (together with James H. Tufts), H. Holt & Co., New York, 1942.
The Philosophy of J. Dewey, selected and edited by J. Rattner, Holt & Co., New York, 1928.
Problems of Men, Philosophical Library, New York, 1946.
The Development of American Pragmatism (in Twentieth Century Philosophy), Philosophical Library, New York, 1943.
A Common Faith, Yale University Press, New Haven, 1934.
Intelligence in the Modern World, J. Dewey's Philosophy, Modern Library, New York, 1939.
Theory of Valuation (International Encyclopedia of Unified Science, vol. II, No. 4.
Ehrenfels Christian, System der Werttheorie, Reisland, Leipzig, 1897-98.
Freeman Ellis, Principles of General Psychology, H. Holt & Co., New York, 1939.
Social Psychology, Holt & Co., New York, 1936.

153

BIBLIOGRAPHY (Continued)

Friess Horace L., Dimensions of Universality in Religion (in Essays in Honor of John Dewey, Holt & Co., New York, 1929.)

Freud Sigmund, Das Unbehagen der Kultur, Vienna, 1929.

Garnett Arthur C., Reality and Value, Allen & Unwin, London, 1937.

Groos Karl, Das Spiel, Fisher, Jena, 1922.

Haering Theodor, Untersuchungen zur Psychologie der Wertung (in Archiv fuer Gesamte Psychologie Bd. 26, 27, Leipzig, 1913.)

Hartmann Nicolai, Ethik, W. de Gruyter & Co., Berlin, 1926.

Heyde Johannes E., Wert, K. Stenger, Erfurt, 1926.

Hook Sidney, A Pragmatic Critique of the Historico-genetic Method (in Essays in Honor of J. Dewey, Holt & Co., New York, 1929.)

James William, Varieties of Religious Experience, Longmans, Green Co., London, 1919.

Jung Carl G., Psychologische Typen, Rascher, Zuerich, 1921.

Die Seelenprobleme der Gegenwart, Rascher, Zuerich, 1931.

Kallen Horace, Value and Experience in Philosophy, Art and Religion, (in Creative Intelligence, Holt & Co., New York, 1917).

Klineberg Otto, Race Differences, Harper and Brothers, New York, 1935.

Koehler Wolfgang, The Place of Value in a World of Facts, Liveright Publishing Co., New York, 1934.

Kraus Oskar, Die Werttheorien; Geschichte und Kritik, R. Rohrer, Bruenn-Wien, 1937.

Laird John, The Idea of Value, Univ. Press, Cambridge, Eng., 1929.

Lange-Eichbaum Wilhelm, Genie-Irrsinn und Ruhm, 2. Aufl. E. Reinhardt, Munchen, 1935.

Lepley Ray, Verifiability of Value, Columbia Univ. Press, New York, 1944.

Lindworsky Johann, Das Seelenleben des Menschen, Bonn, 1934.

Meinong Alexius, Zur Grundlegung der Allgemeinen Wertlehre, Graz 1923.

Fuer die Psychologie und gegen den Psychologismus (in Logos, Bd. 3, 1912).

Montague William P., Belief Unbound, Yale Univ. Press, New Haven, 1930.

The Chances of Surviving Death, Harvard Univ. Press, Cambridge, Mass., 1934.

The Ways of Things, a Philosophy of Nature and Value, Prentice Hall Inc., New York, 1940.

Moore John M., Theories of Religious Experience, New York, 1938.

Otto Rudolf, The Idea of The Holy, Oxford, 1923.

Parker De Witt H., The Principles of Aesthetics, New York, 1946.

Perry Ralph B., General Theory of Values, Longmans, Green & Co., New York, 1926.

Rees Helen, E., A Psychology of Artistic Creation, Teachers College, Columbia Univ. Press, New York, 1942.

Reid Louis A., Creative Morality, Allen & Unwin, London, 1937.

Rickert Heinrich, Zwei Wege der Erkenntnistheorie (in Kantstudien, Bd., 14).

Der Gegenstand der Erkenntnis I. C. B. Mohr, Tuebingen 1900.

Allgemeine Grundlegung der Philosophie, Tuebingen 1921.

Roos William D., Foundation of Ethics, Clarendon Press, London, 1939.

BIBLIOGRAPHY (Continued)

Sachs Hanns, The Creative Unconscious, Sci-Art Publish., Cambridge, Mass., 1942.

Santayana George, The Life of Reason, Ch. Scribner's Sons, New York, 1920.

Scheler Max, Der Formalismus in der Ethik und die Materiale Wertethik, (in Jahrbuch fuer Philosophie and Phenomenologische Forschung Halle a. d. S., 1913-1916).

Schlick Moritz, Problems of Ethics, Prentice Hall Inc., New York, 1939.

Schneider Herbert .W., Radical Empiricism and Religion, (In Essays in Honor of J. Dewey, H. Holt & Co., New York, 1929.)

Simmel Georg, Einleitung in die Moralwissenschaft, Hertz, Berlin, 1892-93.

Lebensanschaung, Muenchen-Leipzig, 1918.

Philosophie des Geldes, Duncker & Humblot, Leipzig, 1900.

Sorley William R., Moral Values and the Idea of God, Univ. Press, Cambridge, Eng., 1919.

Spearman Charles E., Creative Mind, Appleton & Co., New York, 1931.

Urban Wilbur M., Axiology, (in Twentieth Century Philosophy, Philosophical Library, New York, 1943).

Wildeband Wilhelm, Praeludien, J. C. B. Mohr, Tuebingen, 1911.

Wright Williard H., The Creative Will, Lane Co., New York, 1916.

NOTES

1. To the reader who would like to know almost everything that has been said about values, we recommend: Oskar Kraus, Werttheorien, Geschichte und Kritik, Bruen-Wien 1937.
2. Ethics by John Dewey and James H. Tufts, H. Holt & Co., New York 1942, p. 374.
3. Ibid., 371 ff.
4. Sidney Hook, A Pragmatic Critique of the Historico-Genetic Method, p. 162 ff. (In Essays in Honor of John Dewey, New York 1929).
5. The Philosophy of John Dewey, selected and edited by J. Ratner, H. Holt & Co., New York 1928, p. 113.
6. Ibid., p. 119.
7. Ibid., p. 113.
8. Ray Lepley, Verifiability of Value, Columbia University, New York 1944, p. 50 ff.
9. John Dewey, Problems of Men, Philosophical Library, New York 1946, p. 226.
10. W. Windelband, Praeludien, I. Bd. Tuebingen 1911, p. 29.
11. Ibid., p. 42.
12. Cf. John Elof Boodin, Philosophy of History (in Twentieth Century Philosophy, Philosophical Library, New York 1943, p. 91).
13. Heinrich Rickert, Zwei Wege der Erkenntnistheorie (in Kanstudien, Berlin 1909. Bd. 14, p. 181. Cf. his System der Philosophie Bd. I. Tuebingen 1926.
14. H. Rickert, Allgemeine Grundlegung der Philosophie, Tuebingen 1921, p. 27 ff.
15. "At each moment," says Simmel, "in which our soul is more than a mere incurious mirror of reality — which it never is, since objective apprehension is intrinsically bound up with an evaluating of reality — it lives in values, that gather the contents of the world from entirely new perspectives" Georg Simmel, Philosophie des Geldes, 2. Aufl. Leipzig 1907, p. 4 ff.
16. H. Rickert, Lebenswerte und Kulturwerte (in Logos IV. Tuebingen 1911, p. 134).
17. H. Rickert, Der Gegenstand der Erkenntnis, p. 69.
18. H. Rickert, Allgemeine Grundlegung der Philosophie. I. Bd. Tuebingen 1921, p. 262 ff.
19. J. Dewey, The Development of American Pragmatism (in Twentieth Century Philosophy, p. 462 ff).
20. J. Dewey, ibid., 463.
21. The Philosophy of Nietzsche, Beyond Good and Evil. p. 384, The Modern Library, New York.

22. Cf. Ernst Cassirer, Substance and Function, engl. transl. Chicago-London 1923.

23. John Dewey, Problems of Men, p. 222. "If individual cases in experience never gave us any difficulty in identification, if they never set any problem, universals would simply not exist, to say nothing of being used. The universal is precisely such a statement of experience as will facilitate and guarantee the valuation of individualized experiences." ibid.

24. Ray Lepley, Verifiability of Value, p. 78 ff.

25. John E. Boodin, Philosophy of History, p. 95.

26. John Dewey, Problems of Men, p. 222 ff.

27. Cf. Theodor Haering, Untersuchungen zur Psychologie der Wertung (in Archiv fuer Gesamte Psychologie, Bd. 26, 27, 1913.

28. "Every appetite and impulse, however blind, is a mode of preferring one thing to another; it selects one thing and rejects others. It goes out with attraction to certain objects, putting them ahead of others in value. The latter are neglected although from a purely external standpoint they are equally accessible and available. We are so constructed that both by original temperament and by acquired habit we move forward some object rather than others. Such preference antecedes judgment of comparative values; it is organic rather than conscious." Ethics by J. Dewey and J. H. Tufts, New York 1942, p. 316.

29. John Laird, The Idea of Value, Univ. Press, Cambridge, Engl., 1929.

30. Ibid., p. 111 ff.

31. Cf. Wolfgang Koehler, The Place of Value in a World of Facts, Liveright Publ. Co., New York 1934, p. 75 ff.

32. Cf. Th. Haering, Untersuchungen zur Psychologie der Wertung.

33. Ray Lepley, Verifiability of Value, p. 28 ff.

34. S. Alexander, Value (in Bulletin of the John Ryland Library, vol. 17, p. 229).

35. W. Koehler, The Place of Value in a World of Facts, p. 45 ff.

36. Cf. Franz Brentano, Psychologie vom Empirischen Standpunkt, Leipzig 1874.

37. Ethics by J. Dewey and J. H. Tufts, p. 261.

38. Christian Ehrenfels, System der Wertlehre, Leipzig 1897, p. 2.

39. Ibid, p. 65.

40. J. Dewey, Theory of Valuation (International Encyclopedia of Unified Science, vol. II, Number 4, p. 23 ff.

41. J. Dewey, Theory of Valuation, p. 32.

42. Ibid., p. 32.

43. Christian Ehrenfels, System der Wertlehre, p. 37 ff.

44. Ellis Freeman, Social Psychology, H. Holt & Co., New York 1936, p. 123.

45. Ethics by J. Dewey and James H. Tufts, pp. 191, 200.

46. Cf. Ralph B. Perry, General Theory of Value, Longmans, Green & Co., New York 1926.

47. Ethics by J. Dewey and J. H. James, p. 321.

48. Ibid., p. 322.

49. Ralph B. Perry, General Theory of Value, p. 115 ff.

50. Alexius Meinong, Zur Grundlegung der Allgemeinen Wertlehre,

Graz 1923, p. 55. Cf. Alexius Meinong, Fuer die Psychologie und Gegen den Psychologismus (in Logos, Bd. 3, 1912, p. 4.

51. Ellis Freeman, Principles of General Psychology, New York 1939, p. 194.

52. Ethics by J. Dewey and J. H. Tufts, p. 291.

53. Ellis Freeman, Social Psychology, p. 144.

54. John Dewey, The Logic of Judgments of Practice (in Journal for Philosophy, vol. XII, p. 520).

55. Ethics by J. Dewey and J. H. Tufts, p. 312.

56. Georg Simmel, Lebensanschauung (vier metaphysische Kapitel) Muenchen und Leipzig, 1918.

57. Cf. G. Simmel, Lebensanschauung, I. Chapter, p. 6 ff.

58. John Dewey, Experience and Nature, Open Court Publ. Co., Chicago 1925, p. 62.

59. John Dewey, Problems of Men, p. 218.

60. Cf. Wilhelm Lange-Eichbaum, Genie-Irrsim und Ruhm, 2. Aufl. E. Reinhardt, Muenchen 1935.

61. John Dewey, Problems of Men, p. 218.

62. Cf. Johannes E. Heyde, Wert, K. Stenger, Erfurt 1926, p. 25 ff.

63. Max Scheler, der Formalismus in der Ethik und die Materiale Wertethik (in Jahrbuch fuer Philosophie und Phenomenologische Forshung, Halle a. d. S. 1913-1916, p. 414.

64. Ibid., p. 126 ff.

65. Ibid., p. 409.

66. Nicolai Hartmann, Ethik, W. de Gruyter & Co., Berlin 1926, p. 108.

67. Ibid., p. 44.

68. Cf. Chapter I, Value, Desires and Volitions.

69. Rudolf Carnap, Philosophy and Logical Syntax, Paul, Trench, Trubner & Co., London 1935, p. 24.

70. The Philosophy of J. Dewey, edited by J. Rattner, p. 113.

71. Ibid., p. 113 ff.

72. John Dewey, Problems of Men, p. 260.

73. Ibid., p. 241.

74. "Since human life is continuous, the possibility of using any mode of experience to assist in the formation of any other is the ultimate postulate of all science." J. Dewey, ibid., p. 245.

75. Cf. Wilbur M. Urban, Axiology (in Twentieth Century Philosophy, p. 56).

76. J. Dewey, Problems of Men, p. 226.

77. Carnap, Philosophy and Logical Syntax, p. 24.

78. Ibid., p. 24 ff.

79. Cf. Helen E. Rees, A Psychology Of Artistic Creation, Teachers College, Columbia Univ. Press, New York 1942.

80. Cf. Wm. P. Montague, The Chances of Surviving Death, p. 98, Cambridge 1934. G. Simmel Lebensanschauung, Muenchen 1918.

81. H. Kallen, Values and Existence in Philosophy, Art and Religion, p. 409. (In Creative Intelligence, New York 1917).

82. Eugen Bleuler, Naturgeschichte der Seeele, Berlin 1921, p. 34.

83. Intelligence in the Modern World, John Dewey's Philosophy, Modern Library, N. Y. 1939, p. 955.

84. Helen E. Rees, A Psychology of Artistic Creation. p. 121.

85. S. Alexander, Beauty and Other Forms of Value, London, 1933, p. 61.

86. Friedrich Nietzsche, Gesammelte Werke, Bd. XIII, p. 264 (Musarion Ausgabe).

87. Giovanni Gentile, Philosophie der Kunst, Berlin, p. 226.

88. I. M. Guyau, Sittlichkeit ohne Plicht, Leipzig 1909, p. 44.

89. Wilhelm Lange-Eichbaum, Genie-Irrsinn und Ruhm, Muenchen 1935, p. 121.

90. H. E. Rees, A Psychology of Artistic Creation, p. 32 ff.

91. S. Alexander, Beauty and Other Forms of Value, Macmillan & Co. London, 1933, p. 57 ff.

92. Ibid., p. 67.

93. S. Alexander, Beauty and Other Forms of Value, p. 73 ff.

94. C. G. Jung, Seelenprobleme der Gegenwart, Rascher, Zuerich 1931, p. 72.

95. W. Lange-Eichbaum, Genie-Irrsinn und Ruhm, p. 95 ff.

96. Cf. Appendix A.

97. Cf. Karl Groos, Das Spiel, Jena 1922.

98. Lange-Eichbaum, Genie-Irrsinn und Ruhm, p. 119 ff.

99. Intelligence in the Modern World, J. Dewey's Philosophy, p. 961.

100. Cf. Immanuel Kant, Kritik der Urteilskraft, Leipzig 1880. (Kant puts emphasis on the harmonious interaction of sensuous and rational elements).

101. Cf. Williard Huntington Wright, The Creative Will, Lane Co. 1916.

102. Ibid., 247. Wright says: "The perception of beauty necessitates a process of organizing various facts, relationships . . . tracing of sequential lines of form, concentration of shifting of form attention . . . it is almost safe to say that the greater the beauty the longer time it requires to recognize it and to react to it."

103. Intelligence in the Modern World, J. Dewey's Philosophy, p. 977.

104. S. Alexander, Beauty and other Forms of Value, p. 29.

105. . . . merely to feel art is to sink to the plane of the savage, to recognize art by an intellectual process attests to the highest degree of culture man has attained. The ignorant and unrefined live by their instincts, their nervous systems, their prejudices and sentimentalities. The intellectual and cultured man is controlled by constructive thinking, by logic and impersonal recognition of truth." W. H. Wright, The Creative Will, p. 288.

106. C. G. Jung, Psychologische Typen, Rascher, Zuerich 1921, p. 271.

107. S. Alexander, Beauty and other Forms of Value, Macmillan & Co., London, 1933, p. 138.

108. S. Alexander, ibid., 138.

109. Cf. Theodor Lipps, Grundlegung der Aesthetic, Leipzig 1900 (Lipps speaks of empathy (Einfuehlung) as main characteristic of any aesthetic experience).

110. Cf. William P. Montague, The Ways of Things, A Philosophy of Knowledge, Nature and Value. New York 1940, p. 140.

111. S. Alexander, Beauty and Other Forms of Value, Macmillan & Co., London, 1933, p. 172 ff.

112. Cf. Hans Sachs, The Creative Unconscious, Cambridge 1942, p. 157.

113. S. Alexander ibid., 175.

114. George Santayana, The Life of Reason or the Phases of Human Progress, p. 13.

115. Intelligence in The Modern World, J. Dewey's Philosophy, p. 758.

116. Cf. Walter Abel, Representation and Form, New York 1936.

117. Cf. De Witt Parker, The Principles of Aesthetics, New York 1946, p. 82 ff.

118. I. Kant, Kritik der Urteilskraft, Leipzig 1880, p. 73 ff.

119. Intelligence in the Modern World, J. Dewey's Philosophy, p. 998.

120. Ellis Freeman, Principles of General Psychology, New York 1939, p. 483.

121. Alexander overemphasizes the impulses of curiosity and constructiveness in the development of science and art. Cf. Beauty and other Forms of Value, p. 191.

122. Cf. A. Campbell Garnett, Reality and Value, London 1937, p. 257 ff.

123. "Die Kunst und nichts als die Kunst. Sie ist die grosse Ermoeglichern des Lebens, die grosse Verfuehrerin zum Leben, das grosse Stimulans des Lebens . . .

Die Kunst als die Erloesung des Erkennenden, — Dessen, der den furchtbaren und fragwuerdigen Character des Daseins sieht, sehen will, des Tragisch-Erkennenden.

Die Kunst als die Erloesung des Handelnden, — Dessen, der den furchtbaren und fragwuerdigen Character des Daseins nicht nur sieht, sondern lebt, leben will, des tragisch-kriegerischen Menschen, des Helden.

Die Kunst als die Erloesung des Leidenden, — als Weg zu Zustaenden wo das Leiden gewollt, verklaert, vergoettlicht wird, wo das Leiden eine Form der grossen Entzueckung ist." Friedrich Nietzsche, Gesammelte Werke, Musarion Ausgabe, 1920-1928, Bd. XIX, S. 252.

124. Lipps accentuatese the threat of disvalues in our enhanced response to values, which is characteristic of tragedy. "Ich vermag was ich verloren habe nicht nur jetzt zu geniessen, sondern ich geniesse es is gewisser Weise staerker, das es verloren is macht seinen Wert eindringlicher." p. 559, Gruendlegung der Aesthetik. Cf. De Witt Parker, The Principles of Aesthetics, p. 88 ff.

125. Intelligence in the Modern World, J. Dewey's Philosophy, p. 736.

126. Ibid., p. 737.

127. Ibid., p. 739.

128. Intelligence in The Modern World., J. Dewey's Philosophy, p. 739.

129. Ibid., 760.

130. Intelligence in The Modern World, J. Dewey's Philosophy, p. 760.

131. Ibid., p. 730.

132. Cf. Siegmund Freud, Des Unbehagen der Kultur, Vienna 1929. Freud's pessimistic view is based on cases from clinical psychology. Suppressed, inhibited and not converted passions turn

against ourselves, a fact nobody can deny. Freud is wrong in his generalizations which are more or less speculative conclusions.

133. Ellis Freeman, Principles of General Psychology, p. 267.

134. Ibid., p. 237.

135. Ibid., p. 237.

136. S. Alexander, Moral Order and Progress, London 1889, p. 22.

137. Intelligence in the Modern World, J. Dewey's Philosophy, p. 755 ff.

138. Ibid, p. 758.

139. "A man in order to cultivate good health does not think of the pleasures it will bring to him: in thinking of the various objects and acts which will follow from good health he experiences a present enjoyment, and this enjoyment strengthens his effort to attain it. As Plato and Aristotle said over two thousand years ago, the aim of moral education is to develop a character which finds pleasure in right objects and pain in wrong ends." Ibid., 771.

140. S. Alexander, Moral Order And Progress, p. 399.

141. Cf. Moritz Schlick, Problems of Ethics, translation from German by D. Rynin, New York 1939, p. 44 ff.

142. J. Lindworky, Das Seelenleben des Menschen, Bonn 1934, p. 33.

143. S. Alexander, Beauty and other Forms of Value, Macmillan & Co., London 1933, p. 247 ff.

144. S. Alexander, Beauty and Other Forms of Value, p. 260 ff.

145. W. R. Sorley, Moral Values and the Idea of God, Cambridge 1919, p. 69.

146. L. A. Reid, Creative Morality, London 1937, p. 72 ff.

147. W. D. Ross, Foudation of Ethics, Oxford 1939, p. 326.

148. Ibid., 318.

149. W. P. Montague, The Ways of Things, a Philosophy of Nature and Value, New York 1940, p. 149.

150. Cf. A. Campbell Garnett, Reality and Value, London 1937, p. 278.

151. Cf. G. Simmel, Einleitung in die Moralwissenschaft, Berlin 1892-3, p. 8.

152. S. Alexander, Beauty and Other Forms of Value, p. 255.

153. Louis A. Reid, Creative Morality, p. 147.

154. Henri Bergson, The Two Sources of Morality and Religion, transl. by R. A. Audra and C. Brereton, London 1935, p. 7.

155. Wm. P Montague, The Ways of Things, p. 149.

156. John Dewey, A Common Faith, Yale Univ. Press, New Haven 1931, p. 25.

157. Edward Scribner Ames, Religious Values and Philosophical Criticism, p. 3 (in Essays in Honor of J. Dewey, New York 1929).

158. Ibid., p. 27.

159. John Dewey, A Common Faith, p. 25.

160. Cf. Chapter III.

161. Cf. Edgar Sheffield Brightman, A Philosophy of Religion, New York 1940, p. 113 ff.

162. William James, The Varieties of Religious Experience, London 1919, p. 47.

163. Henri Bergson, The two Sources of Morality and Religion, transl. by Ashley Audra and C. Brereton, New Fork 1935, p. 228.

164. Ibid., p. 223.

165. John Dewey, Experience and Nature, p. 406 ff.
166. Ibid., p. 407.
167. Ibid., p. 437.
168. John Dewey, A Common Faith, New Haven 1934, p. 87 ff.
169. William James, The Varieties of Religious Experience, Longmans, Green Co., London 1919, p. 337.
170. William James, ibid., p. 358.
171. Herbert W. Schneider, Radical Empiricism And Religion, p. 343 ff. (In Essays in Honor of J. Dewey).
172. Horace L. Friess, Dimensions of Universality in Religion, p. 139. (In Essays in Honor of J. Dewey).
173. H. Bergson, Two Sources of Morality and Religion, p. 160.
174. Horace L. Friess, Dimensions of Universality of Religion, p. 133.
175. William P. Montague, Belief Unbound, New Haven 1930, p. 33.
176. Ibid., p. 44.
177. Ibid., p. 26 ff.
178. Cf. Rudolf Otto, The Idea of the Holy, transl. from German by J. W. Harvey, Oxford 1923.
179. Cf. Lange-Eichbaum, Genie-Irrsinn und Ruhm, p. 162 ff.
180. John M. Moore, Theories of Religious Experience, New York 1938, p. 72.
181. Edgar Sh. Brightman, A Philosophy of Religion, p. 37 ff.
182. W. P. Montague, Belief Unbound, p. 4. (Cf. H. Hoeffding, The Philosophy of Religion).
183. J. Dewey, A Common Faith, p. 42.
184. Ibid., p. 51.
185. M. F. Ashley-Montagu, Man's Most Dangerous Myth: the Fallacy of Race, Columbia University Press, New York 1945, p. 55 ff.
186. Ruth Benedict, Race: Science and Politics, The Viking Press, New York 1945, p. 96 ff.
187. Cf. Franz Boas, the Mind of Primitive Man, New York 1938. Race and Democratic Society. Julian Huxley, We Europeans, a Survey of Racial Problems.
188. Cf. M. F. Ashley-Montagu, Man's Most Dangerous Myth, p. 55.
189. Cf. Otto Klineberg, Race Differences, Harper & Brothers, New York 1935.
190. M. F. Ashley-Montagu, Man's Most Dangerous Myth, p. 58.
191. Ibid., 188.
192. Gunnar Dahlberg, Race, Reason and Rubbish, Allen & Unwin, London 1942, p. 212.

INDEX

163

ACKNOWLEDGMENTS

The author is deeply grateful to the Committee for Emigré Scholars, especially to its secretary Mrs. Else Staudinger, for a grant which made it possible to complete this treatise, begun a good many years ago. To Professor Horace L. Friess, of Columbia University, the author is indebted for reading the manuscript in its first draft, and for many valuable criticisms. Special thanks are also due to Professor James Gutmann, of Columbia University, for the warm interest he has displayed towards this book. To my friend L. Leo Taub I am grateful for reading the manuscript, and for many suggestions which helped to improve its style.